TAKE YOUR COMPANY GLOBAL

TAKE YOUR COMPANY GLOBAL

The New Rules of International Expansion

NATALY KELLY

Berrett–Koehler Publishers, Inc.

Berrett-Koehler Publishers, Inc.
1333 Broadway, Suite 1000
Oakland, CA 94612-1921
Tel: (510) 817-2277
Fax: (510) 817-2278
www.bkconnection.com

ORDERING INFORMATION

Quantity sales. Special discounts are available on quantity purchases by corporations, associations, and others. For details, contact the "Special Sales Department" at the Berrett-Koehler address above.

Individual sales. Berrett-Koehler publications are available through most bookstores. They can also be ordered directly from Berrett-Koehler: Tel: (800) 929-2929; Fax: (802) 864-7626; www.bkconnection.com.

Orders for college textbook / course adoption use. Please contact Berrett-Koehler: Tel: (800) 929-2929; Fax: (802) 864-7626.

Distributed to the U.S. trade and internationally by Penguin Random House Publisher Services.

Berrett-Koehler and the BK logo are registered trademarks of Berrett-Koehler Publishers, Inc.

Printed in the United States of America

Berrett-Koehler books are printed on long-lasting acid-free paper. When it is available, we choose paper that has been manufactured by environmentally responsible processes. These may include using trees grown in sustainable forests, incorporating recycled paper, minimizing chlorine in bleaching, or recycling the energy produced at the paper mill.

Library of Congress Cataloging-in-Publication Data

Names: Kelly, Nataly, 1975- author.
Title: Take your company global : the new rules of international expansion / Nataly Kelly.
Description: First edition. | Oakland, CA : Berrett-Koehler Publishers, [2023] | Includes bibliographical references and index.
Identifiers: LCCN 2023010700 (print) | LCCN 2023010701 (ebook) | ISBN 9781523004430 (paperback) | ISBN 9781523004447 (pdf) | ISBN 9781523004454 (epub) | ISBN 9781523004478 (audio)
Subjects: LCSH: International business enterprises—Management. | International trade. | Small business—Growth.
Classification: LCC HD62.4 .K455 2023 (print) | LCC HD62.4 (ebook) | DDC 658/.049—dc23/eng/20230322
LC record available at https://lccn.loc.gov/2023010700
LC ebook record available at https://lccn.loc.gov/2023010701

First Edition

30 29 28 27 26 25 24 23   10 9 8 7 6 5 4 3 2 1

Book production: Westchester Publishing Services
Cover design: Ashley Ingram

For my father, Steven Fletcher,
who always encouraged my writing,
in which the lessons he taught me live on.

And for Brian, May, and Eve.
An té a bhíonn siúlach, bíonn scéalach.
(Those who travel have stories to tell.)

CONTENTS

INTRODUCTION

How companies go global has changed. Today, your business is global from the moment you create a website. From that day forward, billions of people around the world can theoretically discover your company, learn about your products and services, and form an opinion of your brand. As a result, the era in which companies focused on just one geography at a time has begun to disappear.

Prominent business leaders and investors are taking note of this phenomenon. In "Global Natives," a study of more than 9 thousand founders and executives of online businesses published by Stripe, the researchers reveal

- 70% of online businesses of all sizes sell outside of their home market
- Of companies with more than 50 employees, the rate increases to 90%[1]

Online businesses were defined as companies that accept online payments, and with online commerce as their primary source of revenue. But online businesses are not only going global at higher rates than other types of companies. They're also doing it much earlier in the life of their business—and with impressive results to show for it. The Stripe report highlights the fact that the companies that expand internationally within the first year of their incorporation have significantly faster rates of both revenue and headcount growth than those who wait until later on (see Table I.1).

Earlier international growth also appears to offer a competitive advantage. While there are differences in growth rates by vertical, the Stripe researchers found that those companies that entered international markets earlier also typically grew faster than other companies in the same category. According to a recent webinar by Stripe, 89 percent of successful tech companies have already expanded into international markets prior to achieving "unicorn" status (a valuation of US$1 billion or higher).

Indeed, a growing number of companies today are not only "born digital" but "born global." The Stripe report also shows that half of the companies surveyed were international from day one. This is possible in part thanks to the growth in online marketplaces, offered by companies such as Amazon, Shopify, Etsy, HubSpot, and many others. These large-scale, global channels enable countless companies to launch their products instantly to a global audience, with minimal barriers standing in their way.

One important takeaway from Stripe's research is that this new wave of business globalization isn't just good for those companies that embrace international growth. This trend actually has the power to boost global gross domestic product (GDP). In other words, increased expansion and commerce across borders isn't just good for individual businesses. This trend may have the potential to grow the world's economy.

The researchers at Stripe are not the only ones who are taking note of this growing and highly promising trend. Partners at Andreessen

TABLE I.1. Earlier Expansion Leads to Faster Revenue and Headcount Growth

Time to Enter International Markets, < 1 year after Incorporation		Time to Enter International Markets, > 1 year after Incorporation	
Revenue growth	+887%	Revenue growth	+746%
Headcount growth	+196%	Headcount growth	+181%

Horowitz have observed this trend as well and have written about what they call the new wave of "Default Global" companies. Unlike "Default Local" firms, these businesses are radically compressing the timeline it takes to go global, often doing it from the very onset of their operations instead of waiting until later. In their examples, a "Default Local" business may take five years before they are operating in a few markets, while a "Default Global" business starts out in a few markets, and rapidly expands into new markets from there onward, and may be in double the number of markets by year three.[2]

Whether you call them "born global," "global natives," or "default global," the concept is the same—businesses that embrace international markets as early as possible often see major advantages. By many measures, the "born global" company is a rising and important trend in business today.

On the other hand, it would be naive to think that borders have disappeared. It's one thing to have easier initial access to customers in different countries. It's quite another to prepare your business to market to, sell to, service, and support them. The internet has broken down what previously seemed like an invisible forcefield. Now, customers from around the world can cross borders, online at least, to engage with your company.

The problem with this new reality is that, in some cases, it can make international expansion even more chaotic and less predictable than it was before. In the past, companies could wait longer, and make more calculated, longer-term bets for expansion. Today, business leaders suddenly find themselves asking many questions at an earlier point in time than they might have expected to, such as, "How much attention should we give to the markets that show strong interest?" "How many markets should we focus on at a time?" "When is the right time for us to grow internationally?" and more generally, "How can we do all this in a predictable and sustainable way?"

International expansion has become both easier and harder. It's easier now to reach customers online, with an app, or through a marketplace, instead of traveling overseas to set up a physical office before you can meet them in person. But in the digital age, it's also harder for many businesses to address the complexity of dealing with customer needs from various countries, at earlier stages of growth, when they are usually still working on finding strong product-market fit.

The good news is that you can become a global company sooner than ever before, which offers tremendous advantages and growth potential for your business. The bad news is, if you're not careful about refining your expansion strategy as you continue down this path, you might end up going into too many markets too soon, before your company is ready. That's why I wrote this book, to help you achieve a balanced approach as you take your company global within this new reality.

Going Global Faster Requires a Global Mindset Earlier

Under the old way of going global, you didn't need to bother with having a global mindset until you were at a more advanced stage of expansion. When founding a company, you could focus exclusively on the vision for your domestic market first, because of the slower pace of going global. From there, you would focus on entering just one or a few local markets at a time, then adding more markets until you eventually became a global business. By the time that happened, you could then focus more people at your company on adopting a global mindset.

Under the new rules, companies need to adopt a global mindset from the beginning, for one simple reason—power dynamics are changing. In the digital age, companies are subjected to more "market pull" than ever before. Customers have more access, and more control, to bring your company into new markets whether this is your strategy or not. And, with the pace of business changing more rapidly today, you need to ensure your company has the capability to intensify your presence in other markets when you decide to pull the trigger and invest more in doing so.

Table I.2 shows how this plays out, according to the old rules and the new rules of international expansion.

TABLE I.2. Old versus New Stages of International Expansion

		Stages of International Expansion			
		At Founding	Early Stage	Mid-Stage	Late Stage
Strategy & operations	Old way	Domestic	Initial market entry	Subsequent market entries	Global business
	New way	Multi market	Local market intensification		Global business
Vision & mindset	Old way	Domestic	International		Global
	New way		Global-first		

Quite simply, the path to building a global business has fewer phases than it did before, which means your vision must be global from much earlier in the life of your company. Without a doubt, the old way worked in the past for building a global company. And there are certainly industries remaining in which this approach may still suffice, even if it takes longer to go global this way. The challenge is that with digitization, international expansion happens not only earlier, but in a much more continuous and ongoing fashion than it did in the past.

What happens if you try to follow the old way in the new era? Unfortunately, there will be a mismatch between your approach and today's reality. Globalization simply becomes harder, because you made choices earlier in the history of your company, without a global vision, that shape your current operations and execution.

If you wait until too late, by the time you get to a place where your vision is truly global in nature, you're likely to uncover too much "globalization debt," much like technical debt, that your company has incurred along the way. In other words, if the choices you make early on are in favor of your domestic market alone, you won't be able to execute on a global vision as fast as you need to in order to keep pace with your industry and your competitors.

However, if you embrace this new reality, creating what I refer to throughout this book as a *Global-First vision* from the beginning, your international expansion will work on turbo-speed and in lockstep with the way business is conducted in the digital age. At a certain point, you may even begin to surpass competitors in market share who were once ahead of you who play by the old rules, because your pace of growth from international markets will propel you beyond them, while you adeptly play by the new ones.

The stages on the path to going global are more compressed now than ever before. Your company might need to stretch itself in ways that don't feel comfortable or natural at times, as you move along this accelerated pathway to going global.

This new approach to going global is not limited to tech companies, the frontrunners of digitization. With few exceptions, this new path to international expansion will eventually become the norm for more and more businesses in every industry with a digital aspect to their business. Other industries tend to eventually follow their counterparts who work in technology down a similar path, as the methods used in tech tend to simply evolve and adapt to the needs of each vertical as time goes on.

Business leaders who seek to future-proof their business, or gain a competitive advantage in their market, are well-advised to prepare for this new reality now. That's precisely what this book is designed to help you do.

The New Rules of International Expansion

Let's briefly walk through some of the outdated assumptions that business leaders held in the past that shaped our thinking about international expansion ("old rules"), alongside the new realities that make those older ways of thinking obsolete ("new rules") (see Table I.3). In the individual chapters that follow, you'll deepen your understanding of these points and why they matter.

TABLE I.3. Old versus New Rules of International Expansion

Old Rules	New Rules
Companies go global after becoming well-established in their home market	Companies can go global as early as day one
Companies need a market entry strategy	Companies need a market intensification strategy
International strategy follows corporate strategy	International strategy is inseparable from corporate strategy
Setting up a local office is critical to expand within a new market	Setting up a local office isn't necessary for initial expansion
Localization is a cost center	Localization is a revenue enabler
Target the biggest markets first	Target the best markets first
Enter a local market, then measure traction	Measure traction, then determine where to intensify
Enter a local market, then adapt your offering	Use the degree of adaptation required to determine where to intensify first
Select a local market, then estimate ROI	Use ROI timeframe to determine when, where, and how much to intensify
Create a domestic strategy, then tweak it for local markets	Recognize that global strategy is the sum of many local strategies
Local teams build a global company one country at a time	All employees build a global company by empowering and enabling local teams
Companies can only have one initial focus market	Companies can have several initial focus markets
People with "international" in their title should lead expansion	Building a global company is everyone's job
Hire for international experience when you get to a later stage of growth	Hire for international experience at every stage of growth
Becoming a global company happens naturally as you expand internationally	Becoming a global company takes intentional focus and commitment
You must grow to a certain size before you go global	Being global is what helps you grow

Chances are that as you read through this list, some of these new rules seem obvious, while others might challenge your assumptions more. This is because taking a company global, especially in this new era in which it happens differently, is not something many people have experience with. Even if you've already worked in international markets in a prior company or job, the conditions in which businesses become global today have changed all around us.

International expansion is ultimately business transformation, which is nuanced and complex. It must be managed across every function of a business, at every level of leadership, and executed across many geographies and time zones. If that sounds challenging, it's because it is!

Everyone knows it's not easy, and as such, the very topic of international expansion often creates many fears. Fear of the unknown. Fear of getting it wrong. Fear of how much there is to learn. Fear of failure. Fear of taking on too much. Fear of stretching too thinly. All those fears are completely valid. And you'll find them to be common among most people at first, especially if they have never done it before.

But along the way, you'll not only be adding international revenue streams. You'll be creating a stronger, more diversified business, and not just for purposes of your balance sheet or your earnings calls, while those obviously matter too. Embracing such a mammoth change initiative and making it a part of the way you operate builds another important muscle. It can help your company become one that continually innovates, incorporates the best of the world's technologies, and has a better read on the pulse of the global market, and your company's and customers' place within it. Once you see your company's global expansion as a business transformation exercise that is imperative for you to achieve your biggest and most ambitious dreams for your business, you can start to approach each international growth conversation from a positive perspective.

In this book, I hope to alleviate any fears you might have by making the unknowns more familiar to you. My goal is to get you excited about the potential of going global and arm you with what you need to succeed at it. As a leader of your business, it's your job to instill a sense of curiosity about what discoveries might await, and to paint the picture of your employees as pioneers who are directing your business on the path to becoming a global market leader. You can do that more easily if you understand not only that the rules have changed, but how, and what it means for your business. In the chapters that follow, I'll be sharing these insights in detail.

This book is the result of many years of learning from local leaders and global colleagues at many companies going global. I have supported many business leaders, both in my past capacity as the Chief Research Officer of a firm specialized in global business, and today, as a colleague, advisor, and friend to many business leaders and investors.

Also, this book is informed, most recently, by the lessons I've learned from working hands on as an executive supporting international expansion efforts, in various roles, and in different business functions, at a large public software company. I've been doing this work in real life not alone, but alongside many colleagues, for the better part of a decade.

But perhaps most importantly, this book comes from a lifelong passion for enabling people to connect across borders of geography, language, and culture. I believe deeply that technology, and the path we're on in the digital age, is well-suited to facilitate a new level of connectedness throughout the world. I've seen firsthand the power, joy, and excitement of bringing new knowledge, new products, and new tools into the hands of people in places that even their creators never expected them to land.

It's a beautiful thing to see a company become a well-known, trusted brand in the most distant locations and in languages the founders and executives themselves do not speak. What could be more gratifying than knowing your business has achieved that sort of reach? It's something I'd love for every business leader and entrepreneur to experience. Fortunately, in the digital age, more and more companies can achieve this. As you'll learn in this book, you don't have to be big to be global anymore.

And even if you're not one of the newer, digitally focused companies that is born global, if you're a leader who wants to take their company global, I'm here to convince you that you have the potential to do so. If there is value in what you're bringing to customers in one market, there is usually value to be found by customers in another. For that reason, even if your company didn't start out with global ambitions, it's never too late to start the journey.

As you read this book, you'll also benefit from case studies with lessons from companies of differing sizes, founded in different places, and at various stages of going global: Airbnb, Canva, Dashlane, Facebook, GoStudent, LinkedIn, Lottie, Netflix, Revolut, Teamwork, and Zoom. Their real-life experiences with going global help illustrate the various concepts shared in the chapters that follow.

So, thank you for embarking on what I hope will be not just another business book in your library, but a fun and enlightening expedition to support you as you bring your company to its fullest global potential in the years to come. After all, no two international growth paths are alike, and each one is as unique as your company. There is no universal map, simple template, or one-size-fits-all framework when you're taking a company global. Instead, there are simply new organizational muscles and skills that you will need to build. Through this book, I seek to help you do that.

And when the valuable products and services you offer begin to reach more people all over the world, I hope you'll come back to me and update me on your experience so I can hear all about your unique path to global success, which will surely be a fascinating one. I'm cheering you on as you take your own company global, and I look forward to hearing about your experience!

I

PREPARE FOR GLOBAL GROWTH

1

UNDERSTAND MARKET INTENSIFICATION

B ack in the old days of international expansion, it was common business parlance to talk about "entering" a new market. This is because companies often had minimal if any customers in a market before setting up a physical presence there. They had to send someone in person in order to go to a country, create a legal entity, set up an office, and start the process of hiring a local team.

Things have changed, on several fronts, but the one common thread is this: international expansion today is much more *continuous* in nature. Let's look at some of the key aspects of international expansion, and what they looked like under the old rules versus the new rules.

Essentially, many services exist today that enable companies to take their business global with far greater ease, and without the need to physically set up operations in each country. For any company with a digital business model, it's possible to "go global" seemingly overnight, as soon as you launch a website that enables someone to make a purchase or offer your company's products through a global online marketplace.

With more marketing, selling, and purchasing happening online than ever before, growing across borders is no longer a matter of a business "entering" a new international market. You can enter dozens of markets simultaneously if you're able to launch a website for multiple countries and access many of the services listed in the "New Rules" column of Table 1.1.

Growing your business globally is increasingly a matter of making choices about which local markets matter most early on, and then intensifying your company's efforts there later, but also being willing to pivot and iterate on your strategy more frequently than you might have had to do in the past.

"Market intensification" is a conscious choice your business makes to go deeper into a market, targeting more local customers, selling more effectively and at a bigger scale, finding the right channels, and further adapting your company's offerings to truly map to local market needs. More and more companies are finding ways to meet customers from many countries where they can all be found initially—online—addressing customers in many markets from the beginning stages of their business.

One major benefit of market intensification is that because it's more continuous, you can more easily adapt and adjust as you need to. You can throttle your speed and invest more or fewer resources in each local market based on factors such as performance, funding availability, and changing economic situations. Overall, under the new rules, you can adjust your international expansion strategy in a much more continuous way, one that is more in keeping with today's ever-changing environments.

Underpinning this transformation of how companies go global today is the fact that the leading technologies today that are modernizing the world tend to be delivered in more continuous ways than in the past. Newer digital offerings that achieve success in today's reality tend to use what is known as a continuous integration / continuous deployment (CI/CD) model.

This fundamental change in how products get delivered in a digital-centric world is not something we can describe as merely "agile." While notions of agility are still important, many people working in software bemoan how far this concept has wandered from its basic roots. One of the core tenets of the Agile Manifesto highlighted the importance of *continuously iterating in response to change* versus sticking to a plan.

TABLE 1.1. Aspects of International Expansion under Old versus New Rules

Aspect of International Expansion	Old Rules	New Rules
Marketing	Required marketers to be located in-country; leaned heavily on local advertising and branding campaigns	Can be done from anywhere in the world; leans heavily on digital marketing and ecommerce
Sales	Sales reps were on the ground in-country and needed to be physically present to meet customers in person	Leans heavily on a remote selling model, online and product-led growth models
Customer support	Required language-skilled staff in-country or at least in time zone, often based in a call center	Highly automated via self-service and with online help content, online chat, and chatbots, e-learning and community forums
Hiring	Necessitated a company to create a legal entity, find local counsel, draft employment contracts and engage a local benefits and payroll provider for each market	Can be outsourced to "employer-of-record" firms that do the set-up work to allow companies to employ and pay people in each market
Product distribution	Was mostly done through local channels on the ground in each country	Marketplaces, mobile apps, web-based, and software as a service (SaaS) distribution models prevail
Finance	Required local bank accounts, local tax specialists and accountants in each country as well as the ability to accept local currency and payments	More countries are instantly accessible via global payment solutions, currency gateways, global accounting platforms, and international tax firms

That principle, which highlights the importance of being adaptable and responsive, is the one I'd like to highlight when it comes to taking your company global. When you build things in a *continuous* way, responding to inputs and customer needs, you need to operate differently. And when you're doing this in multiple markets at once, the need to adjust and pivot in many directions at the same time can feel overwhelming.

For this reason, it's impossible for me to overstate the importance of making sure you truly listen to local customers, create channels to truly hear their feedback in each local market, so that you'll know precisely where you need to flex, in order to make these local market adjustments as continuously as you can.

Talk to your customers in local markets continually. This will help you learn what you need to adapt in order to succeed locally. Use their input to guide where, how, and when to intensify your presence.

Digital Business Models Enable Faster Access to Local Customers

A digital business operating in the current era no longer must make a decision to "enter" a market, as such. Having an online business model means you can open access to many markets at once. Instead, your company will have to make a conscious decision about how to intensify your efforts in markets where you're already seeing early interest from customers.

Companies that have a digital business model have more and more access to the world than ever. However, that comes with less and less control over the exact whereabouts of the customers they initially attract. It's not uncommon for companies to create a website and within a very short timeframe, to have at least 20 percent of their traffic immediately come from outside their home country. This is especially true for companies operating in markets with high levels of demand and strong search volumes for their product category.

Create a website or a blog in a major world language like English, and within a year of steady content creation, you're likely to have visitors from 50-plus countries. As a consultant and advisor, this is what I've witnessed with many companies of various sizes (and even with my own blog).

If what you're selling is in high demand, either because you're in an underlying industry that is growing quickly, or because your product is simply trendy and people love it, you'll be benefiting from viral networks and word of mouth. The world tends to be more interconnected than we think. When people have a great experience with a product, word of mouth can quickly travel across borders.

You'll naturally be pulled toward global markets faster if you have a digital business model, but faster doesn't mean that it will be easier. While you can set up the basic operational mechanics in order to be a global company more quickly than ever before, achieving efficient and scalable international growth has become more complex.

Earlier Global Access Means Introducing Complexity Sooner

While going global sooner is an exciting prospect for many businesses, it's important to recognize the increased level of complexity this can introduce. Many companies haven't yet mastered operations in their domestic country at the point when international business starts to "distract" them. In some ways, strong demand from international customers can be viewed as a "good" distraction, and a sign that a company has a strong chance at global success later. But timing is everything and going into too many markets too deeply before you're ready can do more harm than good. Finding the right balance is critical.

While all the services, platforms, and vendors available can make it seem easy to go global, even if you take advantage of all they have to offer you, here are some of the areas of increased complexity to watch out for anyway in the early days of your expansion:

- **Recruiting.** If you plan to intensify within a market at a large scale, the first hire you'll likely need to make is a local recruiter. You simply can't hire local marketing and sales talent easily otherwise. You might choose to use a local recruiting firm, but then you'll be competing with other clients, agencies may not be able to sell your employer brand to candidates as easily as you can, and it can be difficult to hire at scale without local recruiting. In many markets, candidates also don't want to work for an unproven brand. This is where companies get into a chicken-and-egg situation. They must establish their brand locally before they can attract the best talent, but they can't build their brand until they can hire enough people to market and sell locally.

- **Marketing.** Obtaining more of the desired type of traffic from the right countries, converting it into qualified leads, and ensuring that the pipeline into sales is high quality is a tall order, and can be incredibly hard to scale across languages and countries. The degree to which you depend on digital marketing and a digital business model is the degree to which you are likely to be global without really intending to be. Digital marketing, while the primary strategy for many digital-native or digital-savvy companies, is rarely ever the only one when it comes to demand generation. Often, international marketers end up leaning on more locally differentiated strategies and tactics in order to better reach local markets. Unless you have local marketers for each country or region you're targeting, it can be incredibly complex to manage marketing across several geos at once, until your company is larger in size and has more resources to do so.

- **Sales.** Figuring out how to staff your team, in which time zones and supporting which countries, can be very tricky. Figuring out what their quota should be relative to each market is even trickier until you know for sure what people are willing to pay. And guaranteeing salespeople can meet that quota without having a guaranteed number of leads from marketing in each geo is perhaps the hardest part. A big hurdle for sales teams in local markets in the early stages of market intensification is the lack of local pricing and packaging. Many companies go into these markets without a clear strategy for pricing or even discounting their product. This can make or break a sales team's success in a local market. For this reason, feedback from your salespeople back to product marketing is vital in the early days of building a presence in a new market.

- **Operations and data.** Having a bunch of international traffic on your website before you truly have an international strategy can be confusing. It can put companies in a situation where they either tend to focus on their home country and ignore the rest, or at the other end of the spectrum, get overly excited about too many countries hitting their website and marketing funnel at once. For companies that are eager to grow globally, it can be easy to misinterpret local market signals. Sometimes, metrics may indicate strong "market pull" from a given country that is hungry for what you are selling but might not be a perfect fit for you today due to your lack of a customized local offering.

Depending on your business and which types of outsourced services you choose to use, additional areas of increased complexity that are likely to affect your business early on as you intensify in new markets include: accounting, taxes, billing and renewals, collections, human resources (HR) and benefits, compensation, employment law, mobility, legal and compliance, and more. You don't need to know all the details up front—your company and employees can learn as they go. But it's important for you to know that these are areas where you'll need to give people the necessary time to learn about local nuances and adjust.

Inform Your Strategy with Local Insights and Data

Under the old rules of international market entry, a company had to make a strong financial commitment to a market to even start capturing any data, usually putting employees on the ground to obtain local customer insights, then iterating and learning from there. This process would often take years.

Fortunately, digital companies today that go global sooner than their nondigital counterparts of the past also have a distinct advantage: earlier access to local data and local customer insights. Because they're already in more markets earlier in their history, digital companies can make use of company-specific data and insights to determine exactly where to intensify their growth efforts.

Under the new rules of international expansion, you can analyze performance across several areas to make more strategic decisions about where to intensify. Business leaders can look at key performance indicators in various areas. Looking at data this way requires country-specific reporting, which often requires a certain level of operational and analytical sophistication that many companies don't have until later in their evolution as a business.

Here's the bottom line: If you're at a digital business going global quickly, and you need to figure out where to intensify your efforts, make sure to invest in data analysis and local insights by country as early as you can. Only then can you truly paint a quantitative and qualitative picture of each local market and the opportunity it represents for your business. Otherwise, you'll run a major risk of going into too many markets all at once, spreading your resources far too thin to make any real impact in any one market.

In the chapters that follow, we'll look at how you can mitigate those risks, make clear decisions about which local markets deserve to be part of your growth plans, and understand how to avoid common pitfalls on your journey to becoming a global company.

But before we do that, let's look at one example of a company that embraced going global from its earliest days, not only because its founder wanted to, but because he looked at the data, which made it clear that he would need to go global from the very beginning, in order to achieve his company's business goals.

LOTTIE CASE STUDY
Global from Day One

When Ian Harkin founded Lottie, a toy company based in Donegal, Ireland, he began with international markets in mind from the very beginning. Today, Harkin's business is as global as it gets, with nearly 100 percent of the company's revenue hailing from outside of Ireland. The business reports 60 percent of revenue from the United States, 25 percent from the United Kingdom, and the rest across markets like Canada, Germany, France, and others.

"In the toy industry, with very high up-front development costs, it's difficult to justify that expense to launch in just one country, so we looked at international markets from the very start," explains Harkin, the company's CEO. Launching in many markets at once meant added complexity, but Harkin narrowed the scope to the degree possible: "The path of least resistance for us was choosing multiple markets that speak the same languages. While there will be cultural differences by country, and you still need to work with people in each location, the marketing assets we developed could work across all markets that speak English."

The company had to overcome various hurdles in order to launch across many markets at once. They had to first find a brand name that wasn't already found in the brand trademark registry in each country, in order to protect their intellectual property. They also needed to comply with consumer testing legislation in each country,

(*continued*)

(*Continued*)

which meant paying a premium to go through one of the top international compliance testing houses. "If you were to take a more gradual approach and launch one country at a time, you'd need to pay for testing separately for each country, which would make the cost of testing more than double," Harkin points out.

Because the product was conceptualized for global markets from the start, Harkin and team minimized content on the product packaging, opting for visual imagery instead. "The idea was that if we later wanted to go into countries that spoke languages other than English, we wanted to leverage our packaging while avoiding the costs of translation and packaging redesign work," he explains. The only exceptions were the mandatory safety warnings, required in eight languages, which they added to the packaging globally.

Using a global marketplace was also key to Lottie's ability to quickly build a brand presence and distribution path in many countries at once. "We integrated our store into Amazon, which allowed us to scale operations while outsourcing logistics and customer service," says Harkin. Today, Amazon gives Lottie reach into the United States, Canada, Mexico, Germany, France, Italy, Spain, Holland, Sweden, and Poland. "Using Amazon as a platform enabled us to compete globally from an early stage in the company, so we could focus our efforts on product development and marketing."

Another key factor in deciding whether to launch in many countries at once is knowing your total addressable market (TAM). Harkin knew that the market for toys is notoriously crowded and competitive, with very few segments that grow faster than others. "Focusing on just one country, not even one the size of the United States, would not enable us to achieve our financial goals in the timeframe we wanted," he explains. "For us, going global early helped our product and brand reach more potential customers, much faster than if we would have expanded one country at a time."[1]

Key Takeaways

- Companies today are less likely to enter just one market at a time. Instead, they often enter multiple markets, and then intensify their presence in specific markets later.
- More services and tools exist today to make it easier to go global than ever before.
- However, going global earlier also can add complexity into a business that you'll still need to be prepared to handle.
- Data and insights will be of vital importance to inform your decisions on which markets warrant further investment.
- Using a marketplace to launch a company in multiple markets globally from the earliest stage of a business, as Lottie did with Amazon, is a growing trend, and a viable path to creating a "born global" company.

2

ALIGN INTERNATIONAL STRATEGY WITH CORPORATE STRATEGY

One common question I hear from business leaders is, "How will I know when to create an international strategy?" This varies from company to company, but if one or more of these scenarios applies to you, then you need one:

- You want to accelerate growth using international as a strategic lever.
- You have concerns about your home market economy and want to expand in order to de-risk your business.
- You already have 20 percent or more of your revenue or customers from outside your home market.
- You're a globally minded entrepreneur or business leader who dreams of creating a business with a highly international footprint.

Determine Whether You Need an International Strategy

Here are some helpful questions that you can ask yourself to further determine if you need an international strategy:

- Why do we think we need an international strategy?
  - Does international already make up a large cohort of our customer base or revenue?
  - Does hitting our goals depend heavily on our international growth rates?
  - Do we envision a future in which our business is highly international?
  - Do we think it's important to limit exposure to our domestic market due to concerns about local economic volatility in the long term?
  - Do we need an international strategy today, or at some future point when our international revenue surpasses a certain percentage of our total business?
- Does our international business contain any risks or opportunities for our corporate strategy?
  - **Risks.** Does the profile of our international business look significantly different from that of our domestic business in any ways that are negative (e.g., lower retention, smaller deal size, longer sales cycle, etc.)?
  - **Opportunities.** Does our international business show signs of contributing to our overall goals in a positive way (e.g., improving sales velocity, shifting to a more attractive type of customer, increasing average selling price, etc.)?

Now that the wheels are turning on these questions, let's look at how international growth typically plays out at companies. This will help you understand whether it's necessary to have an international strategy in the first place, and if so, how to align it with your broader business goals.

The Early Days of International Growth at Digital Companies

There are many paths to growing your business, and ultimately, many of them will lead you toward international growth at some point. You can sell more of what you already offer and increase volumes of sales, customers, or both. You can raise prices for existing products, or perhaps add new product lines and sell them to current customers. You can target new segments within your home market based on size or industry. You can explore new sales channels, form strategic alliances or reselling relationships, or grow through mergers and acquisitions. One or more of these classic paths to growth will form part of corporate strategy for many businesses. So, at what point does international strategy become a priority?

For companies at smaller sizes and early stages of growth, international growth isn't usually conceived of as a primary path to growth. However, companies usually trigger international growth simultaneously to pursuing other growth paths, without necessarily having the explicit intention of doing so. In other words, international growth at many companies is a by-product of other actions a company is already taking in order to grow. As discussed previously, thanks to ecommerce and digitalization, businesses today find themselves going global at earlier and earlier points in their business lifecycle.

Many companies take their eye off the international ball in favor of maintaining focus on their other growth strategies. While this is not a bad thing, one risk is that if you don't devote any attention to your international business whatsoever, you might struggle later to align your international strategy with your corporate strategy. At a minimum, you'll want to ensure that your international business does not pose any risks to your broader corporate strategy. In an optimal scenario, you'll want to leverage your international business in order to fuel your overall business growth.

When I talk to most founders and CEOs of businesses with less than $100 million in revenue, I ask what percentage of their customers are outside their home market. For companies located in countries that speak a major global language that is used in multiple continents and economies (such as English, Spanish, French, or German), it's not uncommon for their international revenue to be in the range of 20 to 30 percent. This is frequently true even for early stage or small businesses. In these types of scenarios, a company's international business will usually come primarily from customers that speak the same language as they speak in their home market, giving them a "language halo effect."

If you ask these same business leaders how they got to that stage, they won't usually point to any specific international strategy that led them to this domestic/international split. Rather, they'll highlight the individual heroics of a salesperson, partner, strategic alliance, or small band of enthusiastic people who made their international business possible so far. They see it, at this stage, for what it is at the present moment they're in—a small slice of their greater business.

But what they don't usually think about is how that small slice of today's business could drive their entire company in the future or even give it a turbo-boost. Business leaders at this stage are usually thinking one fiscal year at a time, and don't usually devote much of their time to thinking about how a small international segment might end up driving their entire business five or ten years down the road.

Scaling a business takes extreme focus and energy. Because international is not the primary focus at most small and medium-sized companies while they are in scaling mode, it's extremely rare for companies with fewer than a thousand employees to have a dedicated international strategy. However, it's very common for companies of that size to have a thriving international business with growth that is far outpacing their domestic growth. International strategy usually only enters the picture once a company is already seeing significant momentum, or what is often referred to as "market pull," from outside their home market.

As your business grows, a more advanced question you need to ask is how much of your company's growth—and your ability to meet your overall revenue targets—is dependent on your international business.

Basically, you need to know not only what percentage of your revenue comes from international, but how much uplift your international growth is adding to your overall growth rate. This will enable you to forecast future scenarios, so that you can determine whether creating an international strategy should be a priority.

Let's use a simple example of a company with $10 million in revenue to show why this matters (see Table 2.1). It's not uncommon for scaling businesses to see international growth rates that are double their domestic growth rates, especially in the early years. In this example, the domestic portion of our business is growing at a rate of 20 percent year over year, while the international share is growing at 40 percent (granted, from a much smaller initial base). What happens to the global composition of our revenue, and thus our business, if this pace of growth continues?

By Year 3, if we sustain these rates of growth, the international share of our business will have gained 5 percentage points and will make up 1 in every 4 dollars of our revenue. By Year 5, our international business will make up nearly 1 in every 3 dollars we bring in and is as large as our domestic business was just four years prior. By Year 10, our domestic and international businesses are of equal size, with international set to surpass domestic by the following year.

It's exciting for business leaders to think about how their international business can fuel their overall growth. On a spreadsheet, the numbers

TABLE 2.1. International Revenue Share Can Quickly Shift

	YoY Growth Rate	Year 1		Year 3		Year 5		Year 10	
		Revenue	Share	Revenue	Share	Revenue	Share	Revenue	Share
Domestic	20%	$8M	80%	$12M	75%	$17M	68%	$41M	50%
International	40%	$2M	20%	$4M	25%	$8M	32%	$41M	50%
Global total		$10M	100%	$15M	100%	$24M	100%	$83M	100%

look very appealing to investors and business leaders, and it can be very tempting to lean heavily into international, especially once you start seeing the long-term financial potential. However, a high pace of international growth often comes at a cost that you pay later in terms of operational challenges that you might not envision while you're focused on enabling that very growth.

Table 2.2 shows some common examples of how international growth can start to creep into a business in ways that seem natural and exciting at first. Often, these international growth scenarios seem like good fortune or luck, especially to starry-eyed entrepreneurs who have great ambitions for their company. Indeed, while these are often good signs of market readiness, they can at times be misleading and send your company down a path that creates problems for you and your employees later.

The reason you need to be aware of potential long-term impacts of small actions that happen early on with your international business isn't to dissuade you from pursuing international expansion. Rather, as you intensify your presence in international markets, you can do so with your eyes wide open, as opposed to blissfully unaware.

Don't Let International Become a Distraction

While the idea of becoming a global company sounds appealing to many entrepreneurs initially, sometimes the reality of being a global company, along with all its complexity, can be extremely frustrating, or even too much to handle for a business at certain phases in their development. Here are several common reasons why many executives choose to simply say no to international growth:

- **The timing isn't right.** It's important to trust leaders, especially C-level executives and founders, who have a bird's eye view of where their business is at and where it's headed. No matter how exciting the international opportunity might look, business leaders tend to have a good sense of the overall weak spots in their

TABLE 2.2. Common Triggers of International Growth

Growth Scenario	International Growth Trigger	Future Operational Impact
Word of mouth marketing and referrals	Customers in one country recommend your business to friends and colleagues who live in another country	As the business in the new country grows to represent a larger percentage of your revenue and the local economy changes, customers expect you to account for currency fluctuations
Viral product adoption	A product you develop picks up momentum beyond what you anticipated, carrying you into more markets than you originally planned	There is a growing mismatch between the markets of your customers and the markets that inform your research and development process
Inbound marketing	Thanks to content marketing, SEO, and an inbound marketing methodology, you attract people who are searching online for the types of content you're covering, and they may come from anywhere in the world	Customers begin to find you who hail from economies for which you do not yet offer local pricing or payment options, creating a first impression of your brand as one that is not in touch with their local reality
Account-based geographic expansion	Some of your customers are international themselves and purchase your product for people who may live in different countries	Customers who are part of the same client account may have divergent experiences with your business due to their time zone, location, or language
Super-fans and eager partners	You have fans and partners who bring you into new markets because they are passionate about your company and offerings or want to be first-to-market in introducing you in their country or language	Initial growth in a given market might be misleading and not enable you to scale within that country later
Acquisitions	You acquire a business that has customers in countries outside of your home market	You've added customers in a market that is unfamiliar to your larger business, and they carry a higher risk of leaving, affecting your overall customer and revenue retention

company and whether the timing is optimal to focus on international. Often, international growth is seen by some in the company as a threat at a given point in time. While this can seem like paranoia to international growth enthusiasts, what these leaders have in mind is typically not a desire to say no to international growth indefinitely; rather, they want to throttle it more carefully to prevent the entire car from crashing off the road.

- **There are easier ways to grow.** Many founders and executives are drawn to other types of primary growth paths, such as product-led growth, which tend to be more straightforward. Adding a new product might require repeating a known R&D process, hiring a new sales team, and flexing other muscles that a company has already built and that leaders feel confident about replicating. Many of the underlying business processes that support standard types of growth do not need to be dramatically retooled or overhauled. With international growth, complexity can be higher in many areas.

- **The current pace of growth is already challenging.** While many business leaders seek higher rates of growth and use international as a way to accomplish this, other companies are already in high-growth scenarios and don't want to further complicate an already challenging growth track they're on. Scaling a business quickly, even with underlying market growth to spur you on, isn't easy. Business leaders might be justified, or even wise in many cases, to say that their current pace of growth is just fine. That doesn't mean the opportunity for international growth won't surface soon.

There are variations on these themes. For example, business leaders might state they prefer simplicity, knowing that as a business grows, it becomes harder and harder to keep things simple or remove complexity. Also, the company executives might have prior knowledge of working in a given international market, making them leery of entering it again.

Operational leaders, such as your CFO, COO, and head of people operations, might have good reasons to want to avoid international complexity. Their teams will be responsible for ensuring compliance with local employment and labor laws, dealing with foreign exchange and currency headaches, complying with international accounting standards, and so on. Usually, these teams are the last to be fully resourced when companies are in growth mode, as most businesses place a premium on investments in sales and marketing headcount growth instead, especially in the early years.

You won't be able to align your international strategy with your corporate strategy if you're faced with friction every time you bring up the topic of international growth. One mistake companies make when they have many international detractors is to deny the importance of their international business and assume that if they neglect it, the problem will simply go away. In some cases, it isn't possible to simply give up on international because many of the international growth triggers listed in the table previously are not fully within a company leader's control. Here are some types of detractors to watch out for and how to deal with them:

- **Frustrated super-fans.** You might have employees or partners who are extremely passionate about your business and continue finding success for you in other markets, despite what you as a business leader want to do. So, if the consensus is that you don't want international growth to be a focus area for the time being, you'll need to make this a stated omission and communicate it companywide. Make sure to communicate the time frame to which this prioritization applies, so that employees don't see you as perpetually "anti-global" or "anti-growth." It's not that international growth is off the table; it just isn't your current priority.

- **Wounded veterans.** You might have leaders at the helm of your company who are scarred by past negative experiences with a given market. Be mindful that their opinions of a given country can be highly demoralizing to employees and can even set the tone for future friction. When employees hear things from an executive they admire like, "There is no market for us in France" or "We'll never make it in India," these words can have a lasting impact and sow seeds of doubt that remain, even when business conditions have evolved many years later. Make sure your leaders project an open mind to all markets, potentially in the future so you don't inadvertently communicate that you're closed off to entire populations of future customers. Keep in mind too that some of your employees may have national or cultural affiliations with those communities. Avoid setting a negative tone around any given part of the world where you may someday want to expand.

- **People who are fearful of the unknown.** Many of your employees are likely to be monolingual or have not traveled much outside of their home country. This is especially true for people who live in large countries with plenty of economic opportunity, and where you can build a successful career speaking only one language, such as the United States or the United Kingdom. Don't underestimate how challenging it can be for people to think outside the confines of the country and language that they feel comfortable working within. Often, these folks are the most reluctant to embrace international growth. They tend to think international work will be far more difficult than it truly is. The best antidote for these individuals is simply giving them more opportunities to engage with customers in other countries, until they realize that people are people, everywhere in the world, and that nearly all differences of culture, geography, and language can be overcome.

International growth can generate lots of fear, uncertainty, and doubt for a variety of reasons. No matter why someone is showing up as a detractor, the most important thing you can do is to first recognize the validity of their concerns. If you dismiss their fears or anxieties, they'll view you as someone who simply has no empathy for their fears and doubts. So, hear them out. Let them air those concerns for as long as they wish. Make sure they feel understood. Then, you can try to find common ground that everyone can get comfortable with.

Sometimes businesses can be overzealous regarding international growth and its potential. This too can pose a risk, and usually it takes the form of specific people who are passionate about specific markets. Here are some of the common culprits to watch out for that can derail your company's international efforts:

- **The well-intentioned investor.** Sometimes, a board member or an investor will put in a plug for a given country that can derail the focus of a business. A simple statement, such as "Portfolio Company X has double-digit growth rates in Brazil" sometimes gets interpreted as "come back to me with your fully-baked Brazil strategy." Because boards can in many cases fire the CEO, this can lead some CEOs to feel they need to act quickly on every suggestion. But to protect your business, you must make sure that your international strategy is never shaped solely by the opinions of any one individual, no matter how influential they might be.
- **The copycat CEO.** It's very common for CEOs to study larger companies they admire in order to leverage strategies that have already succeeded. Unfortunately, when it comes to international strategy, this often works against them. They might assume there is something about a given country that makes it attractive, when in fact some other company's past success there might have more to do with the company itself or the phase they were in than the country or market dynamics. Following the market leader can be a good strategy for some companies, but they might also be following a difficult path that, if the larger company could go back in time, they would avoid in hindsight. Don't assume that just because a company you admire went a certain route that it's advisable for your business to do the same.
- **The replicator.** You might also have a leader in your business who wants to replicate success they've seen or even created while at another company, because they have a high degree of familiarity

with that market: "I built a sales channel in Canada in my past company and it quickly grew to 30 percent of revenue, and I can do it again here!" Again, while this might have worked in some other company, it might not necessarily be what is best for your own business. Passionate individuals can be hard to dissuade, and if they are given a high degree of autonomy, they can quickly help your business grow in a country that might not necessarily be aligned with your long-term goals.

- **The self-interested superstar.** As much as we all love to reward our business rock stars and our best employees, if one of your star employees offers to set up an office in another country because either they are from that country originally or they want to live there, be mindful that this might not be in the best interests of your company in the long term. Believe it or not, this is a very common scenario for businesses at earlier stages of growth, and a reason why companies decide to set up international entities. While it can also be a net positive, many business leaders do not realize they are making a long-term business commitment, let alone think about how they will sustain it when their company is 10 times the size. People change their minds a lot, so ask yourself what you'll do a few years from now, when your rock star employee of the moment wants to move to another location or even another company, and you're left with a thriving business in a part of the world that is highly unfamiliar to you, and perhaps not even that desirable in terms of your future goals.

How a Lack of Alignment Affects Top-Line Revenue

What does it really mean for a corporate strategy to be aligned, or not aligned, with your international business? Table 2.3 shows how different levels of alignment can result in missing or hitting a company's revenue target with a new product launch.

TABLE 2.3. Examples of Corporate and International Strategy Alignment

Business Area	Corporate Strategy: Increase Global Revenue by 15 Percent Year over Year by Launching a New Product		
	Alignment with International Business		
	Low	Medium	High
Product development	Company bases the development of the product largely on input from its domestic market only	Company talks to customers in a few key markets and incorporates their insights into development	Company talks to customers in all major markets and languages to create a Global-First product
Pricing and packaging	Company launches an identical product at the same price in all markets at once, but it is unaware that not all markets might value or need the product in the same way as domestic customers do	Company decides based on insights to delay or suppress the launch for certain markets until further product development can take place to increase the value	Company gains a deep understanding of the value proposition in each market, informing the development of adjusted packaging and/or pricing for some markets
Marketing	Central marketing team creates a generic "global" launch campaign that may or may not resonate equally well in each local market, even when adapted, since no local customer insights informed its development	Regional marketing teams adapt the central campaign to better meet the needs of customers in their markets but assume far more work to do this than if customer insights had been woven into development earlier	Informed by local product research upstream, regional marketers can more easily create the best launch campaigns for their markets, leveraging messages and assets that resonate globally with many markets, while applying unique ones that appeal more locally

TABLE 2.3. (Continued)

	Corporate Strategy: Increase Global Revenue by 15 Percent Year over Year by Launching a New Product		
	Alignment with International Business		
Business Area	Low	Medium	High
Sales	Regional sales teams are left with no other choice than to use the generic global messages and training they are given, to adapt the value proposition on the fly, one customer at a time, to help their local customers understand the value	Regional sales teams will be better prepared to speak to the value of the offering, but due to campaigns being delayed regionally, might not have the same ability to hit their targets as sales teams in the markets that informed development earlier on	Armed with locally specific messages, the burden of salespeople is significantly lessened, since the value proposition for local customers has been clearly articulated with the support of marketing, leading to sales acceleration
Customer service and support	Local customers may begin to complain that the value they were promised is not what is being delivered, at least not according to their local perspective, making the job of CS teams much harder	Customers in some local markets may see the value clearly, but others might not, creating additional unwanted burden on the CS and support teams	Because product development was Global-First, customer input went into the up-front product development, factoring in local market needs early. Because the product works well for major markets, the burden of CS and support is significantly lowered.
Year over year growth achieved through strategic alignment	10%	12%	15%+

LINKEDIN CASE STUDY
From Global-First to Global Leader

LinkedIn is without a doubt, a major success story in international growth, with more than 70 percent of its 800-plus million members hailing from outside the United States. International expansion started in the earliest years, from the company's founding in 2003 to 2007. As Aatif Awan, a key leader of the company's international growth in the early years, pointed out in a talk at the SaaStr Annual conference, during those early years, the product was in English only, but because many people in the United States are connected to people in other countries, the network effect took hold, and they quickly reached around 17 million members globally.[1]

Soon after their early Global-First traction began, the company decided to intensify in specific markets. From 2008 to 2011, they translated the website into French, German, and other key languages. Each time they added a new language, they easily doubled their growth rate in that market. Simultaneous to adding more global members, they began creating a global sales team to capitalize on the traction and monetize the growth.

In their third phase of expansion, from 2012 through 2019, LinkedIn intensified even further, seeing massive growth from international markets. They added more languages to increase the number to 24, created dedicated teams to focus exclusively on more challenging large markets such as China, India, and Japan, while doubling down their focus on partnerships for certain key markets.

As the company grew into new markets, making local adaptations became more and more important. They realized that launching a lighter-weight version of the LinkedIn experience would be critical to fuel growth into markets that represented higher future growth than the US market did. They added more local payment options, and importantly, paid closer attention to price. As a general rule, the prices that worked well to grow and monetize in low-income economies were about one third less than for high-income markets.

Twenty years into the LinkedIn story, they have gone through several major phases of growth along the way, but all phases were clearly underpinned by a Global-First mindset, and a focus on not just their home market, and not even on just a few core markets, but a clearly phased strategy and commitment to achieving their bigger global vision.

Key Takeaways

- You might not need a clear international strategy just to get started with global growth, but at some stage you'll need one if you want to truly scale in local markets.
- Make sure you don't prioritize market intensification until your company can give it the attention it deserves.
- Once you have clear goals for your international business, you must align it with your overall strategy, or it won't get sufficient attention from your employees.
- Listen to the concerns of detractors to international growth, but make sure they see how your international strategy supports your longer-term vision for the business.
- Harness the passion of individuals eager to help you grow in a given market, but know that individual heroics today might result in long-term commitments to those markets that later become hard to undo.
- Product development is the fundamental place where getting local customer input matters most, because it has a downstream impact on marketing, sales, customer service, and ultimately your global business performance.
- Take a lesson from LinkedIn and start with a global mindset as early as possible, adjusting your strategy along the way while recognizing the distinct phase you're in, and then intensifying in the markets that will yield the biggest growth opportunities.

3

INTENSIFY LOCAL MARKET PRESENCE

We've made the case that companies are going global earlier than ever. We've discussed the fact that building a successful global business today depends more on market intensification than on initial market entry. We covered the fact that international strategy is no longer a separate path to growth, but that your international business must be closely intertwined with your other plans for your business.

Now, let's look at another factor that has recently changed—the importance of creating a local presence for your business in another country. In today's digital reality, you can build a highly global business and grow it to a fairly significant scale without setting up an entire office, or even a legal entity that enables you to employ people locally, in another country. In this chapter, we'll walk through the reasons why companies still need to set up local offices, despite remote and hybrid work realities.

Essentially, while you can get started with global growth without needing to set up an office and officially enter a new local market, there comes a point where most businesses need to build their company's presence in a local market, or they won't be able to scale in that market further.

There are five main triggers that typically cause companies to set up a local office along their international growth journey. On the surface, these triggers might seem to be the same today, in the digital age, as they were many years ago. However, they tend to happen now at a different phase of a company's growth, and for different underlying reasons. Table 3.1 provides a summary of what these motivations used to look like versus what they look like now.

All the reasons for setting up local entities and offices have to do with one core theme—**access to talent.** Companies usually expand their business outside of their home country to hire people who speak another language, who live in a time zone closer to customers, or in an economy where the employer's costs will be lower.

TABLE 3.1. Reasons for Setting Up Local Entities and Offices

Reason	Old Reality	New Reality
Proximity to customers	Companies required people to meet in person with customers and prospects in order to establish and grow a business relationship	Customers are more comfortable meeting virtually and no longer require as many in-person meetings
Language	Companies hired local talent that spoke the languages of the local market as they set up a new office, when entering the market for the first time	Companies hire people who speak the language, both within and outside of the market, without needing a local office until a certain level of scale is required
Time zone	Due to more traditional work schedules, companies had to hire people who lived directly in the time zone of the customer	Flexible work schedules mean that companies can grow for longer without needing to hire people who live in local time zones of customers
Financial	Businesses would set up offices in other countries to have employees do the same job at a lower cost	Businesses can lower their costs in other ways, such as outsourcing to lower-cost local partners
Mobility	Companies set up a local entity with an expat leader as their first employee to oversee the set-up and future scaling of the local office	Companies create local entities not only for hiring larger numbers of new employees, but to retain or transfer existing employees to offices where they already have local teams

In pre-pandemic times, most companies had a sales model that depended largely on salespeople meeting customers in person. Some businesses, especially those in software and B2B companies, had already begun to develop an "inside sales" model, which refers to selling remotely. In the past, many inside sales teams worked from their company's offices and sold remotely.

When the COVID-19 pandemic hit and many governments began to restrict the ability for people to work in office locations in person, nearly every traditional salesperson suddenly began doing "inside sales," most often from their own home instead of a traditional office environment. Companies that already promoted remote work and inside sales were at a clear advantage. Those that didn't previously do this suddenly had to adapt.

What most business leaders began to realize is that proximity to customers, while offering many advantages, simply isn't as essential as they previously thought. This has led many business owners and executives to ask themselves tough questions. For example, if you can't hire enough qualified workers locally, is it better for your customer to have a more qualified person elsewhere, or a less qualified person nearby? Is it better for you to spend less on office facilities and invest that back into R&D that will ultimately benefit your customers, knowing there is a trade-off between having a team who can collaborate in person versus one that has the additional hurdles of working remotely? What exactly is the value of proximity to customers and employees? And how does the lack of it translate into business results?

The answers to these questions are as varied as businesses are themselves. The "right" answer will depend on many factors, such as the company's views toward remote work, what they are selling, the jobs to be done, and the sizes and locations of their teams. But what we can say for sure is that, thanks to remote work, and because so many companies were forced to gain experience with it due to the pandemic, location no longer matters as much to many businesses as it once did.

When it comes to proximity and how much it matters, a business contemplating an international presence faces a turbo-charged version of this already complex challenge. The idea of supporting customers many thousands of miles away, in a distant place, can seem especially daunting.

Will greater proximity to customers help you grow? If you're already seeing traction in a local market, you probably don't need to go and abruptly open an office there. However, there are several signs that you might want to consider getting closer to your local customers with a stronger in-market presence:

- **Your business requires highly local and up-to-date knowledge.** If your business is dependent on hiring people who have deep and current knowledge of the local market, you'll only find so many of them outside of that geography. While it's possible to transfer such knowledge, certain types of local knowledge evolve rapidly with the local environment. In such cases, you might have no choice but to hire people within a given country versus hiring people who hail from that country but live elsewhere.
- **Your business model depends on highly local networks.** There are times when companies depend heavily on networking to grow. In many cases, local networks cannot be penetrated from afar, and the only chance you have is to hire people locally who are already embedded in those networks or can easily become embedded. In such cases, you might need to hire locally to gain proximity to customers via those networks.
- **You want to invest in building a strong local brand.** Many companies gain a poor reputation when they have foreign employees call on prospects or launch local campaigns without really understanding the local market. They unfortunately don't realize the impact of these decisions on brand perception and word of mouth later. If your brand is important to the success of your business, especially from a competitive differentiation standpoint, or for any

other reason, you'll want to be more careful about managing this locally earlier and with local employees. You can build a brand from afar, but it likely won't be as strong locally in this area as it will if you hire people locally in a given market.

- **You need to better understand the competitive scenario.** There are times when it's faster and easier to simply hire someone in a given market who knows it very well to gain a deeper understanding of competitors than it is to try to glean this information through other means. It depends on many factors, but if you're in a highly competitive space, sometimes getting as close to competitors as you can is helpful.

- **Your business performance is getting worse.** In some cases, you might need to hire locally to scale there and fix performance gaps. Getting closer to local customers might help, depending on the specifics. But beware that simply hiring local employees is not a panacea and could actually make things worse. It's important to pinpoint why certain metrics are off before investing further in a market. Often, local leaders will state that adding headcount is the fastest way to fix local problems, but as we'll discuss more in later chapters, performance gaps are more typically an indicator of a lack of customer addressability, or local product-market fit. In other words, be extra careful about hiring locally when business performance is down in that market.

- **You want to accelerate growth in an outsized way.** The best time to expand by opening an office and hiring more people locally, especially when your investment will be significant, is when business is booming in that market, and your company is hitting most or all of your key performance indicators. However, make sure that your reasons are clear. Is it to have a closer proximity to customers in order to fine-tune your product offering? To refine your local field marketing? To hold more local customer training events? Be sure to pinpoint why and how a local presence will add value, to ensure that opening a local office is the right strategy.

The Very Real Need to Bridge Time Zones

One of the first logistical challenges you will have with supporting customers outside your home country is simply making sure that you can communicate with them during their normal waking or working times. Sometimes, companies get creative by having employees work different shifts and in large markets with many time zones, like the United States, you can cover more geographies from different locations. For example, employees on the West Coast and Hawaii have more time zone overlap with Asia Pacific (APAC) countries, while the East Coast has more overlap with Europe.

Forcing employees to work unconventional hours is problematic and isn't scalable. However, offering employees more flexible schedules can actually be a competitive advantage to the employer when hiring. For example, some employees, especially parents, are happy to work a split shift, which enables them to do early morning work before kids are awake, or late-night hours after their families are asleep. Advertising a schedule as flexible when hiring is important, because it can offer benefits to both the employee and the employer.

You won't be able to scale your company's growth forever based on offering creative solutions like scheduling flexibility alone. How far you can take this type of strategy greatly depends on your pace of growth, and specifically, how many employees you need to hire to cover time zone needs, where you're able to hire them, and for which types of roles. But being more creative with schedules can offer a solution for companies at earlier stages of growth, when you only need to hire one person, or a handful, to cover certain time zones.

Another thing you can do to deal with time zone coverage, especially at earlier stages of growth, is to clearly articulate to customers what your hours of coverage are. This is a simple strategy, but one that often doesn't occur to many business leaders as a possibility. Many companies fall into the trap of thinking that they need to provide full-day coverage during working hours for all customers immediately. Generally, customers are happy with a more gradual approach.

Customers in local markets in the early stages are usually reasonable, and they typically know when buying from a foreign company that you're not yet located in their market. If customers know with certainty that your company's resources or staff are available at certain hours, they tend to appreciate the transparency and clarity. Simply being more explicit can be a path to managing expectations and achieving good results for both your local customers and your company.

TEAMWORK CASE STUDY
Get Closer to Customers as You Scale

For a growing number of businesses, having a global mindset as early as possible allows the company to reap major benefits, but especially when it comes time to scale up. Teamwork, a project management software company built for client work has lived this reality. Founded in Cork, Ireland, in 2007, the company has quite the global presence, with 20 thousand customers in 170 countries, and a growing global workforce of 350 employees in 15 different countries. Nearly all of their revenue is non-domestic (outside Ireland), with 60 percent from North America, 26 percent from Europe, the Middle East, and Africa, and 14 percent from the rest of the world, primarily Australia.

So how did a company just starting up achieve such a global presence? "You can sell software anywhere in the world from the get-go—there are no boundaries. Going global early allowed us to focus on a much larger target market. That said, localizing early can be a strategic advantage in the long run too," says Peter Coppinger, CEO and co-founder.

In the early years, Teamwork focused primarily on English-speaking countries, mainly because of cultural and linguistic proximity. Coppinger explains, "Initially, we didn't have a deliberate strategy, but our product naturally found the most traction in North

America. After a couple of years, we started offering our product and website in the main European languages and getting more traction. Today, we have customers using our product in over 30 languages."

Teamwork is a shining example of the new wave of digital companies that is targeting multiple markets early on in the life of their business to address the broader potential of their total addressable market, but later refining their strategy and focusing locally to gain deeper traction, intensifying in specific markets.

As Coppinger points out, "One of the biggest lessons we learned with Teamwork's international expansion is, in the beginning, you can do it from anywhere, but once you reach a certain scale, you need to get more deliberate about international expansion and targeting the regions with the most potential. Once you know who you are going after you need to develop a strong plan."

The need to develop a more concentrated focus on specific countries to address the needs of those markets more deeply as your company grows is critical. Local laws often drive customer behaviors, even for digital products largely marketed and sold online. "Some of the biggest challenges were posed by legal and compliance requirements and differences across regions (e.g., HIPAA, ISO, SOC, GDPR) that were tough to navigate," highlights Coppinger.

Finding the right talent is also hugely important as your company begins to scale up its presence in local markets. Coppinger and team found that in-market time zone coverage became a key issue as the company grew. "There is no substitute for having staff in the same time zone speaking the same language as your target customer," he observes. "We had Sales and Customer Care based in Ireland for 10 years, but there came a point when we needed boots on the ground in different time zones." Teamwork is headquartered in Cork, Ireland, with additional hubs in Belfast, New York, Toronto, Barcelona, and

(continued)

(Continued)

> Dublin. They recently announced Denver, Colorado, as their new North American hub.
>
> Even for digital companies, there is no replacement for being close to your customers, but especially if you want to grow and expand your relationship with them in key local markets. Coppinger says that the most important lesson for companies going global is to get out there and meet their biggest customers. "Meeting your biggest customers forms a bond for life—customers you visit are 10 times more likely to stay with you and expand. It takes time, but you have to do it."[1]

Hiring for Language-Skilled Talent to Enable Global Growth

One common reason companies open up new offices in other countries is to overcome the language barrier. Different markets have different levels of language proficiency. While it's possible to sell to customers in a language that they learned as a second language, nothing works as well as communicating with a person directly in their language. As a result, many companies grow their presence in a local market without having an office there, and then later expand when they grow to a certain size.

For example, at HubSpot, our first few offices (Dublin, Sydney, Singapore) were primarily English-speaking and offered us greater time zone coverage, but in the case of Dublin and Singapore, they additionally provided access to people who spoke other languages of the Europe, Middle East, and Africa (EMEA) and APAC regions too. We already had customers in many countries at the time we launched offices there, but we knew that we would eventually scale to a point at which we would no longer be able to hire enough native speakers without a local presence. So, the offices we set up in the years that followed were offices where language-specific talent was of critical importance to set the stage for future growth: Japan, Germany, Colombia, and France.

However, don't underestimate how many people you can find who can speak another language even in your home market. If you're in a country with a large percentage of foreign immigrants, you might be able to grow to a certain size just by leveraging the populations that already exist within your borders. For example, you can find large numbers of Spanish speakers in many parts of the United States, numerous French speakers in Canada, and so on. While the exact variant of the language might not be exactly the same as that of your customers, you might not need to open up another office merely to address language barriers with customers in other countries. If you can do this, you can delay the need to "go big" with an office in another country until it's truly warranted.

The Myth of Global English

If your home market is an English-speaking country, how far can you get with international expansion in English alone? English is indeed a global language, but while roughly 13 percent of the world speaks English to some degree, only 5 percent speak it natively. To reach approximately 95 percent of the world in a way that feels native and relevant to them, you're not likely to get very far if English is the only language your company offers.

There is a "halo effect" from most major world languages, because there is a certain segment of every population that usually learns another global language. In some countries, the percentage of the total population you can reach with a major world language can even be quite large. Certain countries, such as the Nordics and Switzerland, have a high percentage of people who speak English with advanced or near-native proficiency, as one example. (I'll share more on the importance of language considerations in your expansion strategy in greater depth in Chapter 8, "Measure Customer Addressability.")

While it's true that you can be an international company and have businesses from many places all over the world using just English, no single language, not even a global one spoken in many large economies like English, will take you past a certain point in your expansion journey. For this reason, most global companies hailing from English-speaking markets will need to add other languages eventually, and vice versa, many companies based in non-English markets must eventually add English too.

That said, you can grow quite a bit within existing foreign markets that speak your company's home market language. The flip side of thinking you can go further than you can with one language is going into too many languages too soon. Generally, neither extreme is good. There are pros and cons to both, but the happy medium for most companies lies somewhere in the middle.

The largest expense category for most businesses is typically their payroll costs, usually followed by the cost of benefits. So, it's no surprise that many companies look to international expansion as a way of potentially reducing their expenses, especially as they grow bigger, and this cost category scales with them.

The concept of outsourcing to lower-cost geographies for financial reasons is nothing new. This trend began in the manufacturing space, primarily to lower the production costs of physical goods. In the 1980s and 1990s, this trend expanded further, resulting in large-scale offshoring of services jobs from places like the United States to India and the Philippines. This model has evolved to include customer support and contact centers, which remain very popular today.

More recently, fueled by the growth of the internet and software industries, companies have tapped into offshoring for purposes of creating engineering teams in lower-cost locations. But what this phenomenon has caused is a realization that the number and types of knowledge worker jobs that people in various parts of the world can do does not need to be limited to just customer support or engineering. More and more types of jobs are being offshored than ever before.

Offshoring is typically viewed as a separate consideration from international expansion, but increasingly, companies are realizing that in markets where they set up offices to reach new customers, by hiring sales and marketing talent for example, they might also be able to benefit from access to talent that is either: (1) less costly than in other markets where they can employ people, or (2) can give them a competitive advantage against other employers competing for the same resources.

If we look beyond traditional offshoring, what is happening more and more, especially in companies with a strong digital focus, is not that they are establishing a local presence in a region with the sole purpose of hiring lower-cost talent. However, lower labor costs do play into their thinking, especially when choosing between various options for where to set up their next office. Increasingly, the strategy a company undertakes for its expansion goals has a complementary consideration, related to the costs of labor and their impact on the company's financial health in the long term as their expansion continues to unfold. Doing detailed financial projections on the various options for selecting an office location, especially in the long term, can result in millions of dollars of additional expense or profit over time.

In companies that highly value their employees, including some tech companies where the competition for talent is fierce, it's not uncommon for companies to create a local office or entity specifically for the purpose of retaining a current employee. In other cases, companies will set up an entity so that they can hire a person with a unique skill set or profile that their business needs. Sometimes, when you find a candidate who is a unicorn with an area of expertise that is highly uncommon, it's worth going to this level of trouble.

Setting up a business entity in order to employ people in a local market is as complicated or as simple as a country's regulations dictate, and this can be a wide spectrum of complexity. Some countries are notorious for making a foreign entity set-up a very difficult undertaking in an effort to give an advantage to local businesses and to ensure foreign businesses make a strong commitment to their market. Others, usually those with development agencies, make it very easy to set up an entity, or even provide strong incentives, in an effort to lure more foreign businesses and keep them there.

If your goal is to intensify your presence in a local market, adding headcount in a local market might seem like the most natural way to do so, especially if you're creating a financial plan in which employees are one of your largest expense categories and the one that always springs to mind. But make sure you don't default into adding headcount just because this is a standard part of your business planning process.

It's important to remember that, especially in the new digital reality, opening up a local office isn't the only way you can enhance your company's presence on the ground in a local market. Here are some other ideas for doing this without going through the hassle of setting up a local office:

- **Do more local customer research.** It's impossible to overstate the importance of communicating with local customers. This is by far the simplest thing any company can prioritize in order to deepen their understanding of local customer realities. The goal is ultimately to create a relationship between your company and local customers. Sure, this can be easier when you're based in the same country or town. But don't underestimate the value of merely having a call with a local customer. Many companies do not measure how often they are communicating with customers, let alone use it to drive local presence. It's one of the most untapped areas of focus that can help drive your success in any local market.

- **Send employees to local markets more frequently.** If you believe it's important for employees to spend time in key parts of the world where your business is growing, you also can send employees there. Keep in mind that you'll need to check local labor laws and ideally work with a mobility consultant to determine what time frame is appropriate. This varies tremendously by country, with local regulations changing quite frequently. Just remember that if the employee does not already live there and isn't from there, you can't compare their experience to that of someone who is truly native and has current contact with the local market.

- **Engage a local partner.** A simple strategy that often works for expanding a company's presence in a given market is to work with a local partner through an affiliate program, a reselling arrangement, a strategic alliance, or some other strategy. Some brands are incredibly successful in local markets without ever hiring a single employee there. Don't overlook this as an option for your company, especially if you already have experience with such partnerships.

If you do decide you need to have employees directly in a given country, you still have other options available to you beyond setting up a local office, such as working with freelancers, or via what is known as a professional employment organization (PEO) firm. Table 3.2 compares some of the options to consider when expanding your company's local presence.

When you open a local entity, the initial burden can be very high for your core operational teams. You'll need to add local payroll, local accounting and tax specialists, local benefits, local legal support, facilities support if you have physical office space, and much more. Often, you can accomplish some of these things via third-party firms and global agencies, but even so, your core operational teams are always affected with each entity you add.

Freelancers offer significant advantages. They can enable you to establish a presence in a local market without many up-front costs, and without creating additional burden for your core operational teams, such as

TABLE 3.2. Options for Expanding Local Presence

	Freelancers	Agency	Local Corporate Entity
Operational burden	Low	Medium	High
Management burden	High	Medium	Low
Up-front costs	Low	Medium	High
Long-term costs	High	Medium	Low

payroll, benefits, facilities, and IT. However, when you get to a certain scale, freelancers can present a burden for the people managing them day-to-day who have to track their hours, approve their invoices, review their work, re-train them, and so on. The main challenge of working with freelancers is that you cannot guarantee a long-term relationship with them, thus making it hard to scale any function this way over time.

Intermediaries, such as agencies, often provide a happy medium for many companies. They can enable your business to scale in local markets, but usually at a higher cost in the short term. For many companies, the price is very much worth paying during a certain phase, to fuel growth and drive revenue that can be directed back into funding further investments in revenue generation and growth. Indeed, if your business succeeds, you might well outgrow the need for intermediaries rather quickly. While you can outsource many business processes to third parties, keep in mind that the decision to do this will likely be one of a legal nature, so check with your legal counsel or legal advisors before undertaking any such business relationship to ensure it's the right path for your company.

If you have a very strong culture at your company, and you believe you'll be building hubs in various parts of the world that serve as local "founding teams" in each market, you might need to invest directly in hiring employees from your earliest days of expansion. There can be strong benefits to doing this for your long-term growth. Those founding teams tend to absorb your culture more readily and can reinforce and strengthen each other to build your new local business. Freelancers and contractors require less up-front investment but might not feel as invested in your company or aligned with your culture in the long term. It's also important to think about how you'll retain these local members of your team. Ideally, you want people who will have a hunger not just to do a job for your company, but to actually help you grow for the long term in a given market.

When businesses are in a high-growth phase, they focus on the local markets that seem to offer the most opportunity and focus particularly on sales headcount growth. They may also focus on hiring for other customer-facing teams that will be most obviously impacted beyond Sales, such as Marketing, Customer Service, Training, and Support.

However, what business leaders often lose sight of in the excitement of so much growth is the additional pressure their expansion plans can add to already overwhelmed operational teams. Operational teams tend to be less vocal and push back less, because the CEO and other key leaders during such phases are usually inspired by the momentum the company is seeing, not to mention being charged with ensuring the company grows and interfacing most often with board members and investors.

Here are some of the teams and subteams that can be most affected during these phases of global growth:

- Finance
- Accounting
- Payroll
- Renewals
- Collections
- People Operations
- Human Resources
- Benefits
- Recruiting
- Training
- Culture
- Legal
- Corporate Counsel
- Mobility
- Employment Law
- Risk Management
- Security

International expansion is often driven by Sales. But make sure to support all the other teams who will likely undergo stress and feel they are being pushed outside the bounds of their knowledge, bandwidth, or both. There is a steep learning curve for each new market a company enters with intention of scaling, so give your teams time to adjust and absorb the new information they'll need in order to do their jobs and expand their teams to meet local needs. It also takes time for them to build relationships with vendors locally and globally to support the new offices.

The Importance of a Local Launch Playbook

When you initially decide that your company should set up a local presence in any new country, it's time to take action and make it happen. Many companies realize very early in their international expansion efforts that the steps you must take in order to set up full operations in a new market follow the same basic pattern around the world. At the most basic level, here is what most companies end up discovering with their first launch:

- To hire people in a given country, you first need to have two key fundamental pieces in place: the ability to hire people and the ability to pay them.
- But in order to hire someone, you'll need a local legal counsel who knows the employment laws of each country and can draft your employment contract and other key legal documents you'll need.
- To pay people, you'll need to set up a bank account so that you can actually move funds to a local market in order to pay your employees there.
- Before you can set up a bank account as a business in most countries, you'll often need a local entity, and you might also need a person to go in person to set up the bank account. Sometimes, this can be done by your local legal counsel. In other cases, it might need to be an employee of your company.
- To make sure you stay in compliance with local employment and tax laws, you'll have to hire people (either as contractors or

employees) who can ensure you're doing what is legally required in each country on both fronts.

- To make your company attractive as an employer, you'll also need to offer benefits in each country, depending on what is covered by a government's system: health care, paid parental leave, retirement savings, and so on.

If you want to sell into a new market, and your business model requires you to hire salespeople or other positions, the steps above are the basics that you'll need to cover before you can hire your first local employee. Because some of these steps are interdependent, it's ideal to have someone with a project management mindset who can take care of running them all.

Every company needs to create a playbook unique to their culture and business. However, most of the playbooks that I've seen from different countries cover essentially the same steps. So, Table 3.3 shows some tasks you can use as guidance for building your own local playbook. While this list might appear to be long, it only covers the basics of the things you need to think through when deciding to set up a local entity or office in another country. Your ultimate list will depend on your company, who does what, and how you decide to go to market in each place.

Beyond these core tasks, here is a list of somewhat more advanced questions you may wish to think through as you're planning for your local office launch, so that you can work them into your playbook if they are relevant for your company.

1. What advantages can we offer in the new market as an employer brand?
2. Will there be a local office launch event, and if so, who will coordinate it?
3. Who will be our local office leader (general manager)?
4. Will we send any expat employees from our HQ country to the local country?

TABLE 3.3. Major Task Areas for a Local Launch Playbook

Who	What	Notes
CEO, Sales Leader, Ops Leader	Assign a Program Manager to run the overall launch process	Choose someone who can work with all functional leaders, and who is familiar enough with all parts of your business, to manage all the steps involved
Finance	Decide what the financial targets are	Come up with some basic targets to hit in your first year at least
Finance, Sales, CEO	Decide how much you want to invest	Look at how this will affect core metrics (profitability, lifetime value/customer acquisition cost, etc.)
Sales, HR, Recruiting, Finance	Determine how many people you will hire, when, and in which roles	Make sure as you create your plan that you consider it may take you longer to hire if you're unknown in a new market. Find out what the average notice period is and how long it takes to recruit.
Recruiting, Facilities, HR	Decide where you'll put these roles	You might decide to place some roles in the new market while keeping others in an existing market instead. You'll need to ensure you have space for them if you're giving them the option to work in an office.
Recruiting, Finance, HR	Decide who will recruit for you	Look at whether you want to handle recruitment directly or through a local or global agency
Legal, HR	Determine if you'll be setting up a local entity or going through an agency	Consider whether your growth plans are rapid or slow. If rapid, you may outgrow an agency in a few years.
Program Manager	Create the launch timeline	Time line depends on the number of people you're hiring. Setting up a small presence can be done in three to six months in most countries.
Marketing, HR	Determine public relations plan	You might pre-announce the office and associated headcount if you have multiyear growth plans

TABLE 3.3. (Continued)

Who	What	Notes
Program Manager	Engage the Local Development Authority	Build a relationship with the local development authority in your target country and find out what resources they offer to companies starting up a new presence there. Examples: Irish Development Authority in Ireland, Procolombia in Colombia, or JETRO in Japan.
Finance, HR	Create a multiyear headcount plan	Create a simple plan for at least the first 12 to 18 months of headcount growth after launch, so Finance can use this for modeling impact on the rest of the business
HR	Select a benefits provider	Your company's existing global benefits provider might offer local options or partner with a local benefits provider
Legal	Contract with a local counsel	This person in the local market will advise the company on all matters including initial entity creation
Finance	Decide where to create a bank account	Some banking providers have international branches, but many do not. Decide which bank you'll be working with.
Finance, HR	Decide who will handle local payroll	Your finance and HR teams will need to determine who to work with for local payroll provision
Finance, Legal	Decide who will handle local taxes	Your accounting team may opt to outsource to a local firm or to work with a global provider for managing your corporate taxes
Legal, HR	Draft local employment contract	Your legal team along with your HR team will need to work with local counsel to ensure you understand local implications and nuance. Some countries will require you to issue the contract in a local language; others may require a courtesy translation to be offered to employees.

(continued)

TABLE 3.3. Major Task Areas for a Local Launch Playbook (Continued)

Who	What	Notes
Legal, Product	Draft and/or adapt other legal contracts	Beyond just the employment contract, you may need to make changes to your global legal docs to comply with local law. For example, perhaps you have a master terms of service agreement, but the laws in a new country have different requirements. This may change details of how your product is provided to customers. Again, you may or may not be required to translate these.
Finance	Decide if you'll add any new currencies or payment methods	You may decide you want to collect revenue in a new currency to offset your cost basis in the new local currency. Or you may decide to keep things in just one currency.
Systems and Infrastructure	Add any new currencies and payment methods	If so, you'll need to work with Finance to plan for these, and with IT to enable them in your billing, reporting, collections, and so on
Sales, Ops	Remap sales territories	If you're taking the new country out of an existing territory for your sales team and adding it to a new one, you'll need to remap these in your systems, reporting, and sales plan
IT, Engineering	Update data storage and transfer processes	Depending on what new data you'll be collecting from the new local market, you may need to revisit your data architecture along with storage and transfer processes
Finance	Update invoicing and billing	Make any changes required by local laws and taxes on the invoicing and billing side
Facilities, IT	Begin search	If people will work in offices, your facilities team will need to find a local office, look into access/security, and coordinate the build-out with desks, computers, etc.
IT	Plan for IT coverage	Decide whether your IT team will support employees in the same zone
Localization	Determine localization needs	Decide whether you'll be offering a localized website or will localize any of your product or service offerings in time for the launch

5. If so, what are the visa requirements, tax requirements, and other implications for the expats?

6. How long will the expats stay and what will be the hand-off process for local leadership?

7. How often will key executives visit the local office?

8. How will local employees engage with the HQ office?

9. How and where will we train new hires?

10. What does the financial plan look like, including all estimated costs of salaries, facilities, third-party costs, legal costs, and estimated quarterly breakdown?

11. What is our plan for generating brand awareness?

12. What are the targets for the sales team to hit?

13. What are the related lead flow targets for marketing to hit?

14. By when will we have to hire each new headcount to ensure we minimize risk to the financial plan?

15. What is the estimated "time to payback" on the initial investment?

16. How will we ensure ongoing communication between the new local hires and HQ?

17. Who will support local employees, and will the reporting structure be local or international?

18. How else can we make sure local employees stay connected to and participate in our corporate culture?

19. What will we do if some of the new hires in the local office do not work out?

20. Do we have a clear plan for what to do in the event of local political unrest, a natural disaster, or some other unexpected events that could derail our operations?

21. What if the expats we chose need to return to their home country for some unforeseen reason?

22. Do we have all the target metrics broken down into monthly goals for Year 1?

23. How will we ensure that we have a clear local view of all core metrics that matter companywide for this market?

24. What are the leading indicators that we will not be able to deliver on our plan?

25. What do we do (back-up plan) if we see early warning signs that we will not succeed?

26. What is our risk mitigation strategy if we do not hit our targets?

27. What is the tolerable margin of error on our core target metrics?

28. What payback period would we consider a success?

29. Do we have the cash flow to continue funding the local operations if we don't succeed?

30. What is our maximum runway in terms of months, dictated by our current cash flow and trajectory?

31. What would be the conditions under which we would decide to pull out of the market?

32. How flexible can we be in terms of resources to re-adjust the plan with minimal impact?

If this list seems daunting to you, please don't let it be. In reality, most companies are not able to answer such a comprehensive list of questions before they set up a local office. A big part of the international intensification process entails significant organizational learning. So, many of the answers to these questions are uncovered by the people who are leading the local office launch process and supporting international expansion efforts. This is basically the "homework" they'll have to complete to make an office launch happen.

Most companies don't even know what questions to ask when they go about launching an office, which is why they all end up building a playbook at some point to capture what they learn so they can accelerate the launch process and do it better each time around. The decision to launch is already made, after all. Of course, you can jump straight into it and begin checking off tasks, building a playbook unique to your company as you go. However, walking through some of these questions can fast-track your company and help you jump the learning curve. This can lead to quicker success on the ground in your target market, for whenever you decide to set up a local presence there.

When you develop your international office launch playbook, you'll also want to create a cross-functional launch team, a clear timeline with all major steps required in every functional area, flagging dependencies, work streams, and all the specific tasks and deadlines to move through each phase. From security to facilities, from bank accounts to benefits, from re-structuring sales territories and adhering to local tax requirements, to coordinating public relations and throwing a launch party, and everything in between, each item will need to be tracked and managed by a member of the operations team.

With each of the new offices you launch, you'll learn new things and adjust your playbook accordingly. Approximately 80 percent of the items required to launch in each market are the same tasks, only with constantly changing stakeholders to engage with, both internally and locally. With each new office you add, there are new things to learn, and additional complexity of course, which comes with being a global company.

AIRBNB CASE STUDY
Early Expansion via Acquisition

Founded in 2007, Airbnb is widely known for its global success. What many might not know is that only three years into its existence as a company, it made a rather bold and unconventional move, acquiring a small competitor in Germany with a similar offering called Accoleo, and thereby launching into Germany. By 2011 when the acquisition took place, the company already had 60 percent of its revenue generated outside the United States. From that point on, Airbnb quickly began to intensify its presence in Europe, with international growth being an important focus ever since. The company

(*continued*)

(Continued)

opened up offices not only in Hamburg where Accoleo was located, but in Berlin, Munich, and Vienna as well.[2]

Two of the biggest benefits for Airbnb of getting feet on the ground in key local markets within Europe so early were: (1) organizational learning and (2) local brand awareness. Organizational learning is hugely important for companies going global, and tremendous amounts of growth took place during the company's early expansion years in Germany and other countries within Europe. This helped them get to where they are today with more than 4 million Airbnb hosts who have welcomed more than a billion guests into their homes worldwide. Local brand awareness is incredibly important too, and even back in those early days of expansion, Airbnb focused on building strong relationships with local hosts to boost brand awareness and help spread the word.

As the Airbnb experience demonstrates, sometimes acquiring a local competitor in a key market, even in the earliest years of your business, can be a great way to force organizational learning company wide, helping the organization build muscles for global growth that it will need to flex later on. Also, don't underestimate the power of people on the ground, and employees who know the local market, to become passionate advocates for your company and fuel local brand awareness. Ultimately, all companies are made up of people, and all successful global companies are made up of people from many parts of the world.

Key Takeaways

- Most businesses set up a presence in another country for five reasons: proximity to customers, language, time zone, financial reasons, or mobility reasons.

- If you attempt to do everything in just one global language, such as English, your growth will slow down at some point.
- You have options for setting up a presence in another country: freelancers, agencies, direct entity creation. Your choice will largely depend on how fast you want to scale.
- Don't underestimate the significant burden that creating a large presence for your company in another country will create for your operationally focused teams.
- You can leverage much of the same playbook you create for one country to expand further into another later, but the process of intensifying your company's presence will change with each new market you go into and requires continual updates as you grow.
- Don't overlook acquisitions of companies in local markets as a strategy not only for growth, but for gaining international experience while fast-tracking organizational learning on what it takes to become a global company.

———— CHAPTER ————

4

ENABLE REVENUE WITH LOCALIZATION

What is localization, and why do you need to pay close attention to it as you take your company global? In this chapter, we'll cover what localization really means, why it's so often misunderstood, and why it matters so much for your business as you're expanding internationally. We'll also cover why you'll want to play a major role in driving it for your business.

The term "localization" is often thrown around in conversations about international expansion, but for many business leaders, localization is an elusive area that isn't covered in management courses or in business school. Yet, it's a vital part of international growth for any company, so it's important for you to know what it means and why it matters for your business.

Localization means adapting an experience for a local market.

The experience aspect of localization is critical. Ultimately, the goal of localization is to enable an excellent customer experience for customers in a local market. Yet, localization is rarely connected at most businesses to the teams or executives in charge of customer experience, even though this is the heart of its very mission. Ironically, localization is also usually disconnected from market research, which is also central to enabling high-quality local experiences for customers.

The origin of the term "localization" does not really come from "going local" as many tend to think. It also does not mean "taking your business into a local market," nor does it mean simply "adapting your business model for a local market," although it's sometimes also used in these ways. People who are more familiar with localization use the term in a very specific way, because it has a specific meaning in the tech field where it originated. The term "localization" actually comes from a technical concept first introduced in the software field, known as a "locale." A locale merely consists of the standard codes for a language and a country. Table 4.1 shows some examples.

Because of its genesis, professionals who work in localization are trained to think about adapting an experience for both a language and a country. It's important to highlight this, because when you ask them to "localize into Spanish," many localization professionals will naturally ask you, "for which country?" They're not trying to annoy you, but rather, to clarify so they can do the job at hand. Spanish is a language, but they need to know the locale. Similarly, if asked to "localize for Canada," localization folks will ask, "into which language?" In localization, geography and language have interlinked importance. In some cases, a locale can also be used to designate a language combined with a grouping of countries or a larger geography—for example, localizing an experience

TABLE 4.1. Examples of Locales

Locale	Language	Country
en-US	English	United States
en-CA	English	Canada
fr-CA	French	Canada
fr-FR	French	France

into Spanish for customers in Latin America, or into German for customers in Germany, Austria, and Switzerland.

What many business leaders are not aware of is that, because international expansion is so common, localization is actually a vibrant and thriving profession. While it's a niche and specialized area, many people working in business are often surprised to learn that there are numerous college degree offerings, and even graduate degree programs, in localization. In that sense, it's similar to many other professions that you typically find in tech-driven and digitally minded companies (engineering, product development, and so on). It tends to attract people with international experience, but who also have an interest in both languages and technology. In other words, localization leaders can prove tremendously helpful to your company as allies, advocates, and key drivers of international growth.

Localization is also a big business. It's an industry that has been around ever since software began and forms a large part of the language services and software market, which is valued at anywhere from US$50 billion to US$70 billion, depending on the source. Many business leaders don't realize that localization is a very developed professional discipline, and that there are more than 30 thousand businesses globally that offer these types of services, with many tens if not hundreds of thousands of professionals engaged in this industry who are prepared to help you with it.

I've met many leaders who assign someone at their company with no background in localization to the task, and just expect them to figure it out. If you're thinking about doing that, please at least surround those newbies with plenty of people who already have ample experience in this area. They can fast-track your company and prevent you from making common mistakes and learning the hard way.

Successful Localization Depends Heavily on Associated Processes

The degree to which localization is successful depends squarely on several other processes that must occur either before it, or alongside it.

TABLE 4.2. Simplified Definitions of Core Adaptation Processes

Process	What Gets Adapted
Localization	Experience
Translation	Message
Internationalization	Code
Globalization	Framework

Table 4.2 offers simple, one-word definitions of localization and its associated processes to help clarify what localization means, but also, what the associated processes mean.

As your company grows internationally, you might run into some "numeronyms."

__L10n__ is an abbreviation for localization, and __I18n__ is an abbreviation for internationalization.

The numbers 10 and 18 simply represent the number of letters in between the first and last.

Translation is a common part of most localization projects, so this is another process that it's helpful for you to know a bit more about. One common misconception among businesspeople is the idea that translation means converting words from one language into another. If only it were that easy! If so, anyone could translate using a dictionary or a free online translation tool.

Translation means adapting a message for a local market.

To localize an experience, messages also typically need to be adapted from one language and culture to another, which is known as "translation."

What you're adapting when you translate properly isn't words, but rather the message or the meaning. If you translate words alone, the meaning typically gets lost, thereby ruining the message. So, meaning needs to be adapted as part of the translation process to ensure it resonates properly and can be understood fully.

Interestingly, many businesspeople expect translation to be faster, easier, and cheaper than it is in reality, because they tend to assume that translation technology is much further along than it actually is. Automated translation tools exist, and they are constantly improving, but human translators still play an important part in translation projects for most business purposes today, and likely will for the foreseeable future. Even in cases where language professionals are only involved in setting up and training AI tools, this still requires deep knowledge of how the tools work, and the know-how to access professionals in the translation space to ensure the quality of such tools continually improves. Translation, or adapting a message created in one culture so that it will resonate properly in another, is an exponentially more complex undertaking.

Most business leaders, especially monolingual ones, become frustrated or surprised when they learn that translation isn't as easy as just clicking a button. Technically, you can take a website and translate it automatically with no involvement from human translators whatsoever. Just like you can also transcribe your thoughts into an email and automatically send it to your customers. The question is not whether you can do that, but whether you should. In fact, doing so may get your website flagged by search engines and harm your rankings and traffic using current algorithms, although these are continually evolving.

Increasingly, automation and AI will be part of every company's standard translation toolkit. Yet, your company needs to employ these tools for the right settings and content types. There is nuance to figuring out your localization strategy, of course, which localization professionals can help you navigate.

While translation is a part of most localization projects, there are times when it's not necessary. For example, let's assume we're adapting an experience for users in a local market who speak the same language, but need to pay in another currency, or use different forms of measurement. There are certainly many instances in which localization does not require any translation at all, but rather, requires adaptation of design, imagery, and other elements instead.

Adapting any web-based or software experience relies on code to work properly, so that the right local variants can be displayed. The process of adapting the code to ensure that localization can happen successfully is referred to as internationalization.

Internationalization means adapting code to enable localization.

Commonly, businesspeople also use the term "internationalization" much more broadly, in the sense of "to take something international," but when localization practitioners use it, they're actually referring to making changes on the code side of things so that localization can technically happen. So, if you hear someone ask, "Is that software internationalized?", what this essentially means is, "Can this experience be localized?" Technically, what it means is that the underlying code was written in a way that enables the experience to be adapted for additional languages and geographies.

The earlier internationalization happens, the better. Trying to internationalize after a product is built is much harder than building it with global in mind from the start. It requires huge amounts of refactoring, which engineers and product teams dislike. Product teams love extensibility but failing to build internationalization into development early on is the very definition of limiting extensibility.

When internationalization doesn't take place, localization becomes painful at best, and impossible at worst. Localization teams are often the bearers of bad news to executives, explaining that a given website, tool, or app will take tremendous engineering resources to "redesign" to enable localization. Engineering resources are precious and finite. This means executives are often presented with an ugly choice: "Should we have our developers build something new that most of our customers want and need, or should we have them spend their time rearchitecting something older, to enable us to improve the experience for a subset of our customers?"

Most business leaders will naturally choose to build something new that benefits the majority of their customers. Product leaders also need to keep engineers engaged and excited about the next cool thing they get to build. When this option is competing with an alternative that means fixing something that shipped a long time ago to most customers, for engineering, it basically means fixing someone else's legacy code and going back to do boring and demoralizing clean-up work. No good manager wants to have their team spend time on that.

This is the classic scenario in which an ounce of prevention is worth a pound of cure. The problem with internationalization is that engineering resources are so valuable that no one is willing to spend a pound of cure later, because every ounce they spend will actually have more impact elsewhere for the business. For this reason, the sooner you can make internationalization a priority for your business, the better. That way you can avoid facing a conflict of interests between meeting the needs of the majority of your customers and meeting a different set of needs for your international customers only.

Lastly, the term "globalization," while used more broadly, tends to mean "taking something global." But for localization practitioners, it has a much more specific meaning. It means adapting the underlying framework to ensure it's global-ready. The lack of globalization is one of the most challenging things localization teams deal with. When something wasn't built with global in mind from the start, at times it's actually impossible ever to properly localize it.

> *Globalization means adapting a framework to work for multiple local markets at the same time.*

Usually, when localization fails, it's due to dependencies that relate to internationalization (code problems), translation (language problems), or globalization (problems with the underlying framework). What do we mean here by "framework"? Table 4.3 shows an example of a business framework, before, during, and after globalization.

Now, in this example, you can imagine that localization might also play a part. Well-intentioned leaders might say, "Let's translate all our support content in Hindi, this should help our customers in India!" But that might not be necessary or advisable. If the customers are already engaging with this business in English, it could be confusing to suddenly make support content available in a language that the product is not even available in, and that your customers are not accustomed to seeing from your business.

Business leaders often try to solve gaps in the market that they see reflected in other metrics by merely throwing projects at localization. What is often needed isn't yet another localization project, but rather, someone who can take a step back and look at the situation from the perspective of the local customer.

If you can see the customer's local reality by stepping into their shoes temporarily, you'll quickly spot where the gaps are and how to fix them. However, this takes a willingness to step outside of your own local comfort zone and actually talk to the customer. It also takes an ongoing awareness that the frameworks you create at your company are usually based on one local reality, that of your home market, and therefore might not be suited to another local reality in a different country, culture, and economy.

Most often, when businesses start to see major problems with their business metrics in a given local market, they turn to the idea of investing more in localization, but rarely take a hard look at whether the

TABLE 4.3. Examples of Adopting a Framework for a Local Market

	Before	During	After
Business situation	70% of our customers have historically been based in the Nordics, where the cost of labor is high and human involvement is not expected. We have not been targeting international growth, but domestic growth has slowed down.	There is strong interest and a big market for our product in India, which has grown to 10% of our total revenue in recent years and fueling our overall growth. But we are starting to see customer retention numbers dive and growth slowing down there.	Our retention numbers in India are now nearly at the rates of Nordics, and our growth has accelerated in India again. Now India makes up 12% of our business, and we are leveraging our new framework for other high-growth markets with similar profiles.
Framework	We deliver customer service in a highly self-service manner. Our customers do not want to be routed to an intermediary or a human; they want quick and easy answers online that enable them to self-serve. This has worked extremely well in the Nordics where we are based.	Our framework does not include a strong human component, but this is expected in a market like India. In the Nordics, only 10% of customers need to consult with a human. Our customers from India are highly technical, but rates of human involvement are in the range of 50%. Our support team is overloaded, and we cannot provide sufficient coverage for time zones or for the growing volumes.	We engaged a third-party outsourcing firm in India who support our Indian customers using a local cost basis, but our customers in Nordics also have better access to human support now too for more complex needs, and at a lower cost than before. We are now reinvesting the savings in sales and marketing to target more businesses in India, and in other priority markets in Southeast Asia.
Result	A framework that was designed based on the needs of just the company's home market	A framework that is not flexible enough to map to a local market with different needs	A framework that not only addresses local market needs, but benefits the country's home market and overall business

underlying framework could use some simple adjustments to enable it to be more global friendly. When you spot such problems, you can do a few things:

1. **Consult with your localization professionals.** Ask your internal team, or if you outsource this work, ask your external localization providers. Ask whether there is something off with the underlying framework itself. They are usually among the first to spot what's broken.

2. **Ask the employees who are closest to your local market.** What are they hearing from customers? What would work better for customers instead? Often, the voices of employees who serve customers in local markets need to be amplified.

3. **Talk to customers in your local market.** This is by far the best way to find out what you should do differently. Ask for feedback, especially from the customers who are the unhappiest. They often have the most helpful feedback.

Now that you understand what localization is, and what the different associated processes are, let's look at who the people are within a business environment who stand to benefit the most from localization, as well as the people who can influence localization most positively, and how a lack of successful localization can harm their overall productivity and business outcomes.

There are four groups of people who have a vested interest in making sure localization is successful. Let's take a look at each, and why proper localization matters for them and impacts their work (see Table 4.4).

Localization Directly Impacts Customers and Prospects

The customers who pay your company are the ultimate stakeholders that localization and its associated processes all seek to serve. As a result, their

TABLE 4.4. Examples of Adopting a Framework for a Local Market

Process	What Gets Adapted	Key Stakeholders
Localization	Experience	Customers & prospects
Translation	Message	
Internationalization	Code	Developers
Globalization	Framework	Employees

input is paramount, and ensuring they have a delightful experience is imperative. When localization is poorly done, your customers can directly suffer, as can your company's relationship with them.

If their experience is negative, it might slow them down significantly or prevent them from accomplishing the goals they set out to achieve via your products and services. Ultimately, poor localization stands in the way of a relationship of trust between your company and your customers. If localization does not succeed, your business might not actually be living up to its promise to them.

If you are doing any sort of localization for marketing purposes, there is tremendous risk involved if you don't ensure localization happens successfully. Like the new kid on his first day of school, you do not want your company to have a poor first impression in a new market, because it can set the tone for how you are perceived from there on out, and impressions can be hard to change once established.

In some ways, prospective customers in local markets hold even more power than existing customers in local markets do, because they help define your future and set the tone for further expansion. Customers who are already in a contractual relationship with you obviously have tremendous value to you, but you also offer value to them, and this exchange of value is already known and accepted. Obviously, retaining these customers is hugely important, and localizing their experience will help you continue to keep and ideally grow those accounts.

However, if your business is dependent on continually winning net new business in new local markets in order to hit your financial targets, your relationship with local prospects has the potential to make or break your future. Prospects in local markets who end up saying no to you at the last minute can harm your close rates, your quarterly results, and your annual financial targets. If you're a public company, they can even affect your share price and investor confidence.

It tends to be harder to convince prospects to take a chance with you than it is to build on or renew a relationship. This is especially true when you're just starting to build a brand presence within a new local market. Take a look at the percentage of all net new leads or opportunities your sales team can close in a given local market. Now, compare it to the rate at which you retain or grow your customer accounts in that same local market, which is usually higher. For this reason, localization for marketing purposes tends to be extremely high stakes.

As discussed, when defining internationalization, developers are the ones who get hit with problems when localization isn't set up for success, and this can ultimately impact the health and growth of an entire install base. Software engineers despise the drudgery of having to go through old code someone else wrote, only to clean it up or rewrite it, to make it work for new markets. It's painful work, and many will deem it simply not worth the hassle. Yet, many development teams are asked to do this awful task.

What ultimately happens is that companies that realize the importance of this type of work in hindsight, in the best interests of international customers end up driving away the engineering talent they need to grow their business. So, it becomes a difficult choice. Do we demoralize our engineers to serve these customers and possibly fail other customers who are waiting on other things? Or do we solve the needs of these local customers who are in markets that are fueling our future growth?

Unfortunately, the only way to solve this is to make internationalization a true priority for developers as early as you can. Otherwise, you'll later be faced with this exact challenge of choosing between demotivating your engineers and delaying other customer needs or deprioritizing your international customers. Neither of these is a good choice, so it's critical to prevent this scenario by planning for it!

International Employees Face Friction When Localization Fails

It's clear that customers suffer when localization fails, but what happens to your employees when localization is not successful? Quite simply, most of the burden falls to them, and you'll make everyone's job harder than it should be. It also isn't just your international employees and your local leaders who end up picking up the slack, although they are the ones who tend to feel it most acutely. The pain of ignoring globalization is typically felt companywide.

If you adopt a Global-First mindset as early as possible, all of the processes that help you adapt your business for local markets later—localization, translation, internationalization, and globalization—will happen faster and with less friction.

If you care about building a strong employer brand, retaining your best talent, and growing them over time into leaders so you can build a sustainable organization, you should continually ask yourself whether you're doing enough to drive Global-First at your business. You don't want your employees to feel the stress and friction that manifest later on, simply because you haven't built things with a global mindset early on. Your employees will inevitably start to feel friction and complain about this disconnect if Global-First is not an important tenet of your culture, one that you can see play out in everyday interactions and decisions.

Because localization impacts customers and prospects so directly, it clearly influences, and in fact enables revenue. It also impacts many different parts of the internal workings of a company, and the employees who work there. As a result, globalization ultimately is the job of more than just the localization team. It's everyone's responsibility, companywide,

TABLE 4.5. Key Influencers for Enabling Business Adaptations

Process	What Gets Adapted	Key Stakeholders	Influencers
Localization	Experience	Customers & prospects	Sales, Marketing, and Customer Success Leaders
Translation	Message		
Internationalization	Code	Developers	Product and Engineering Leaders
Globalization	Framework	Employees	CEO and Executive Team

to ensure that localization can succeed. Table 4.5 shows the primary influencers who need to advocate for successful localization, alongside the key stakeholders.

Often, businesses think they're successful with localization if their international business is doing well. Growth rates seem good initially, sales hiring has strong momentum, and the numbers look good. In initial phases of market entry, the picture often looks rosy for companies, especially if they're hitting the early adopters for what they're selling in a given market. This is when you might think all engines are firing and your business is doing splendidly in a given part of the world. Unfortunately, early financial success in a new market can be both misleading and short-lived.

To keep your company's growth going in a local market, you need to focus on more than just those initial indicators. You need to ensure your localization is truly successful, continuously. Unfortunately, successful localization isn't something you can easily spot. Most companies invest a lot of energy and resources in localization but have no idea if they're successful with it or not.

To understand if your localization is successful, ask your customers how you're doing at serving the needs of businesses in their country and language.

The only way to know if you're succeeding with localization is to ask your customers for feedback. For that reason, you'll need to measure local customer experience on an ongoing basis so that you can see not only where you stand, but where you need to make improvements.

Whatever you do, don't assume that "completeness" of localization is a proxy for localization success. This is a trap that many companies fall into, and it can be a dangerously misleading one. Many business leaders think you can achieve localization success by merely listing all the pieces of content or software that comprise a customer experience, and then measuring what percentage of them are localized.

The fault with this thinking is simple. Not all customers need the same things. If you localize everything, you'll be wasting valuable time and resources on localizing things that aren't necessary, or even perceived as helpful by your customers in other markets. Instead, you'll need to figure out what truly is mission-critical to customers in each market, so you can focus your resources on delivering that instead—whether it's through localization or native strategies. Usually, a combination will be required.

If you often find it difficult to connect the dots between localization and international expansion, you're not alone. Nearly every business leader I've ever consulted with knows that localization is important to their overall strategy, but the picture of where exactly it fits can seem murky. Table 4.6 illustrates why this connection often seems so difficult, and why, when we start to include internationalization and globalization, it gets even more confusing.

TABLE 4.6. Visibility of Processes Enabling International Expansion

Most visible	Expansion
	Translation
	Localization
	Internationalization
Least visible	Globalization

When you think about the internal airtime that the different business processes related to international expansion receive, expansion, because it's measured in revenue, usually is something you talk about frequently. The executive team focuses on revenue every year and quarter (or monthly and even daily depending on your business model). If you work at a public company, revenue is reported for the world to see. As you go global, your international revenue becomes more visible, making expansion something you talk about more frequently.

After your company's international revenue, translation is typically the next most visible area of focus for companies going global, and a topic that seems more accessible. Anyone can tell if a website or product is translated into another language, but unless you're bilingual, your visibility is limited, and you can't necessarily know *how good* the translation is.

One layer deeper down, we find localization. This is where things begin to get muddled for most business leaders. Only a customer from a local market can truly determine if an experience has been adapted properly to meet their needs. Most companies fail to measure this or to ask their customers about their local experience, so often localization becomes a black hole, with no one in the company able to determine if localization is "good" or "bad" or something in between. As a result, localization is talked about very rarely by business leaders.

If we go a layer deeper, we find internationalization. Localization cannot be successful when code isn't internationalized to enable experiences to work properly. Only developers have exposure to this layer and the ability to impact it, but business leaders are usually quite disconnected by the time we reach this degree of detail.

And at the very bottom layer, we find the least understood area of all, from which everything else in your company stems—globalization. If your company isn't operating from a global framework to begin with, here's the series of events that plays out invisibly, in this order:

- **Globalization isn't prioritized.** Company leaders focus on international expansion, but not on globalization, assuming globalization will happen naturally as a result of more international revenue. Because it's not a stated focus, it's at the back of employees' minds, but never the forefront.

- **Internationalization gets ignored.** Why should product teams and developers care about building for global growth if it isn't a company priority? If it's not a part of the company core, and a strong focus, it's easy to see why internationalization gets sidestepped in favor of other initiatives.
- **Localization is hindered.** If the code and systems won't support a local experience, localization is set up for failure. Localization teams will often do what they can, but their hands will be tied due to choices that were made further upstream.
- **Translation suffers.** When localization can't be done properly, translation usually takes a hit as well. Companies might only be able to translate content partially, and can't provide an interface in a user's language, for example. The translation, without the right context, won't make much sense, which turns into wasted resources and poor brand impressions.
- **International revenue slows.** If your company is providing a poor experience and people get a bad impression of your brand, growth in a local market can slow or stagnate. Often, companies don't see the true root of the problem and try to make surface-level changes to fix things. Sadly, they are also usually unaware of how good their international growth could be if only they fixed the deeper problem, the lack of a Global-First mindset.

Layer after layer, if you look deeply enough, you'll see that your company's long-term success with international expansion ultimately hinges on globalization. Therefore, it's up to you, as a business leader, to ensure that your employees hear, early and often, how important it is for each of them to have a global mindset while building a global company.

Sometimes, other teams will point to localization (either the process or the team) as the reason for problems that emerge with the bumps and bruises of international expansion. But problems typically occur because the underlying framework isn't global, and because there was no Global-First mindset informing that framework when it was first developed. Leaders must use their megaphone to repeatedly talk about the importance of building a global company and globalizing from within to enable the expansion that occurs as a result.

To ensure localization can make a sufficient impact on your organization, it's important to provide strong functional representation at the highest possible level of leadership that makes sense for your company. This sends a message that localization is something you're committing to for the long haul, as a strategic priority for your business.

While it's not common to find localization leaders in executive roles at every company, there are a growing number of large public companies with individuals in Vice President (or at least Director) roles who are leading the charge with localization and globalization for their businesses.

Speaking from my personal experience, the question of where localization sits within the company functionally is less important than ensuring two things: (1) strong alignment between localization and other teams, and (2) giving localization ongoing access to key leaders at the company, ideally an executive role. Without access to executives, localization leaders can struggle to support overall company strategy and build the alignment they need to ensure the entire organization can achieve true local success.

When the localization function reports to an executive leader, it means that localization is more squarely on the radar and can be more readily intertwined into strategic planning and goal setting at the highest levels of the company. For companies that are not as large, what is more important than a mere title or role is the level of access that your localization leader has to other leaders at your company. In general, if you have a less hierarchical organization, access to executives might not be a major barrier for localization teams in the early days of your company's growth. But as time goes on and your company gets bigger, it becomes more important for localization leaders to have visibility and access to executives to do the things that help your company achieve global success.

If you seek to scale your business into a large and highly global one, you'll want to ensure that localization can play a vital part within the cross-functional team that enables continued expansion and the overall globalization of the business.

FACEBOOK CASE STUDY
Accelerating User Growth with Localization

For any business leader who wishes to understand the power localization offers a company to intensify their growth in new markets during the scale-up years, there is perhaps no better example than Facebook. Back in 2007, when the company had only 450 employees, Facebook began enabling its users to translate the interface, quickly launching many languages in succession. By 2008, the company saw tremendous growth in many markets where the languages were spoken that they could attribute directly to these early localization efforts.

The user growth numbers of those early days of Facebook are remarkable and speak for themselves. Facebook saw their user base in France jump from 1.4 million to 2.4 million in only three months. Likewise, users in Italy moved from 375,000 to 933,000 in just four months. This language-fueled growth trend kept playing out in key focus markets for Facebook, but also had spillover effects in other places around the world where users spoke those languages.[1]

Today, Facebook has billions of users in more than a hundred languages. What's important to keep in mind is that localization is never a "one-and-done" exercise, but rather the beginning of a long journey forward into a new market. Think of initial localization as a great way to fuel your growth but be mindful that it can also serve as a tipping point at which your business will need to start offering richer and better experiences to customers in a given language. This is usually where things become far more challenging.

Now that Facebook is available in so many languages, including many minority languages that are not widely resourced, new challenges emerge for the company around content moderation, auto-detection of hate speech, and other linguistic signs of problematic behavior, for which monitoring tools often do not even yet exist in many languages.[2] Not all languages have equal value to a business, and it can be difficult to justify making major investments in long-tail languages, especially as businesses get larger and their growth begins to slow.

Facebook's experience is a good reminder that while localization can be hugely impactful to drive growth in early phases of scaling in new markets, as you go deeper into those markets, things will get more complex. In later phases of new market penetration, it becomes even more important to keep your eye on the full picture of user experience, ensuring that where differences arise, you know what the key issues are and how to address them, using localization as one of many tools in your company's toolkit.

Key Takeaways

- Consciously choose to view localization as a driver of international revenue and not as a cost center.
- Make things easy for your employees by clearly defining localization and the associated processes. These terms have very specific meanings but can easily confuse people.
- Know that localization is a big industry worth many billions of dollars, and that there are plenty of people out there with deep knowledge in this area you can easily access and hire.

- When complaints arise about "localization," challenge yourself to look at the underlying framework, which is usually where the opportunity lies to make the biggest, monumental improvements for your local customers.
- As the experience from Facebook shows, localization can serve to fuel the growth of your business and help you scale, but also becomes a more complex undertaking as you go deeper into new markets.

II

DETERMINE WHERE
TO FOCUS

5

APPLY THE MARACA MODEL

For many businesses, figuring out where to focus can at first seem over-whelming. You will hear lots of opinions from people both inside and outside your company about what constitutes a "good" market. Your internal data might lead you to focus on certain countries, while third-party research might contradict what you're seeing on the ground. There's no doubt that figuring out where to focus can initially be a daunting task.

The purpose of the MARACA framework is to clear this fog. It can provide a clear, at-a-glance view of the relative value of a given country to your business compared with others, in order to facilitate international strategy decisions and help you prioritize. If your international efforts are just starting, it can help you shortlist the best markets. If you're already doing business in other countries, the MARACA model will help you figure out where to intensify further.

I first developed this model when I began running international operations and strategy at HubSpot, but it largely draws on my experience as a business consultant for global companies. Because I wanted to help companies at an earlier phase in their business evolution, I published the model in an article in *Harvard Business Review*,[1] hoping it would reach more business leaders so that their companies would not have to keep reinventing the wheel.

It seemed to strike a chord. Since its initial publication in HBR, and a subsequent webinar with HBR, the MARACA model has been used by many companies to help guide their international expansion decisions. What's useful about this model is that it's highly customizable and flexible. No two businesses are the same, so no two expansion strategies should be either—not even for companies operating in the same industry.

This next section of the book is designed to expand on the model and help you understand it more deeply, beyond the basics covered in the HBR article, so that you can leverage it for your own company. In this chapter, I'll cover the basics of how the model works, so you can learn how to apply it at a high level. In the chapters that follow, I'll break down each section of the model in greater detail, with clear examples of how to put it into practice at your business.

Use Models to Inform, Not to Prescribe

Before we dive in, here's one important caveat. While I hope the MARACA model will prove helpful to you, it's important to remember that there is no perfect answer to questions of going global and which markets to target in which order. All you can do is make an educated guess and commit to your decision, evaluating your progress as you go.

The reason I don't want to oversell any model, not even one that I created, is that the environment we live in requires agility and adaptability. Strategies must evolve along with the changing needs of your customers. International expansion takes time, but it's not just a long-term commitment. It's an enduring and continuous one. Once you start down the international expansion path, it shapes the trajectory of your business for as long as your company exists.

For this reason, international expansion planning cannot be looked at as a one-time exercise, but rather, must be viewed as a continuous and ongoing part of your business operations and strategy, one that you revisit frequently. Entire economies, societies, industries, and markets can change rapidly, and so can your business. For this reason, consider any model or decision-making framework as nothing more than a basis for plotting your company's initial destinations. There is absolutely no GPS, turn-by-turn guidance system for international expansion, because there is no final destination. Your company will have to keep driving and navigating the roads toward many different places, for as long as you remain in business.

And while you can and should attempt to learn from people who have traveled on those roads before, know that not all of their experiences will be exactly like yours. You're driving a different vehicle, with different passengers, on a different day, with different road and weather conditions. For this reason, while I'm a big fan of companies engaging with international advisors and consultants, I also don't believe you should rely too heavily on those opinions alone. Remember, no one is more of an expert in your business than you are.

No one knows your local markets as well as your customers and employees do. Their voices, over all others, should guide you fundamentally. I firmly believe their views will offer you more insight and value than any sort of model or framework ever can, no matter how great the data that informs it.

With all this said, most companies do find it helpful to have some sort of framework, if only as a starting point to help them think through their options. That's why I came up with this one. For companies that don't already have a strong point of view on how to choose markets to expand or intensify into, the MARACA model is one that can flexibly meet the needs of most companies.

Not every company needs a model to clarify their thinking on going global. You might already have a strong perspective on where your company should go next, and where to intensify. But if you don't, or you need to further develop your reasoning for going into a given market, consider using this model as a way to test your assumptions and make your thinking crystal clear.

Focus on Countries, Not Regions

You'll often hear US-based business leaders in the early years of their international journey make statements like, "We've made our first EMEA hire," or "We're doing well in APAC." While regions are helpful for sharing broad trends, they also mask individual country differences that might be driving the broader regional trend. As businesses become more mature in their expansion efforts, they get more specific and start to talk about countries instead.

Europe is not a market. It's a region made up of many countries, all of which are markets in their own right. Every region and subregion is made up of distinct countries, and these countries can vary widely in their ease of access and opportunity. Having greater granularity about the specifics of each country gives you the ability to improve your focus. The MARACA model's focus on countries, as opposed to regions, is important. Focusing on countries, not regions, will help steer you in the direction of becoming a more mature global operator sooner.

Because the MARACA framework will ask you to look at your key metrics by country, I strongly encourage you to set up your data in a way that enables you to see things in the following ways:

- **Country view.** How is this country performing compared to others? How does it compare to our domestic market?
- **Regional view.** How is this region performing compared to other regions? How does it compare to our domestic market?
- **International view.** How does our international business perform compared to our domestic business?
- **Language view.** How do countries that speak this language perform compared to others? How does performance in this language compare to performance of countries in the language of our domestic market?
- **Tiered view.** How do our top focus markets perform compared to markets on which we focus less? Many companies end up tiering

the top countries that make up the majority of their business, placing other countries that are less of a near-term priority in different tiers.

One of the things you'll want to prioritize is making sure your data structure includes a consistent list of countries, aligned to the geos and sub-geos that you likely already have in place at the company for designating sales territories. You may also wish to add the primary language for each country, so that you can easily group countries by their primary language, to enable reporting with that view too. This will help you make localization decisions more easily later.

You should standardize your company on a consistent geo and language-specific data infrastructure as soon as possible with the people in charge of your systems and tools. If you don't, you'll face a giant mess on the data front later on, in which every system you use tracks countries and geographic information differently, requiring all sorts of manual clean-up that is time intensive and can slow your company down.

For example, you'll see just one country show up in your reporting at least five different ways: "Great Britain," "the United Kingdom," "U.K.," "UK," "United Kingdom" (without "the"), and so on. Make it a priority to work with your data analysts to get your company onto a standard country list mapped to your company-specific geo definitions, along with languages. When you fast forward a few years out, it will be very easy to add these fields into any other reporting, so you can access geo-specific and language views of your information with relative ease.

It might seem tempting to simply lunge into a market that seems good to you based on common sense. Many company leaders, especially entrepreneurs and founders, are no strangers to making impactful decisions based on little more than their business instincts. While you can do that, you won't get the benefit of one of the biggest advantages of going global in the digital age: data. Companies with an online or digital aspect to their business have access to more data than ever before, and having this perspective can change which countries you decide to prioritize.

A simple model that many companies use looks at markets from the most basic perspectives, asking two key questions: (1) "How big is the market?" and (2) "How easy will it be for us to do business there?" Those two questions are essential, but if you're lacking the third dimension of data on your company's local market traction, you will essentially be driving your business into a new country with a broken speedometer. Without any ability to measure your current speed at any point in time, you cannot forecast how long it will take or how fast you will succeed. MARACA consists of three dimensions and includes this game-changing data layer. By taking advantage of the insights your company's data can offer about new local markets, you'll be able to reduce the risk of your expansion efforts and make decisions with greater confidence.

Three Metrics Help Summarize Market Attractiveness

The MARACA model is made up of three areas that, in combination, can tell you how attractive a market is for your business at any given point in time (see Table 5.1).

We'll talk more about each of these in depth in the chapters that follow. Before we do, it's important to understand why you need to look at market attractiveness from these different lenses.

With market availability (MA), you'll get a sense of how big the market is. Real-time analytics (RA) will help you gauge how your company

TABLE 5.1. Definitions of the MARACA Components

	Metric	What It Tells You	Why It Matters
MA	Market availability	How much **opportunity** does this market offer?	Size ($)
RA	Real-time analytics	How are we **performing** in this market?	Traction
CA	Customer addressability	How **easily** can we address this market?	Timeline

is performing in that market at any given point in time, which is critical since local markets, business trends, and macro environments can change rapidly. And customer addressability (CA) is perhaps the most important, because it will give you a relative idea of how long it's going to take to achieve success in the market. When you score each area, you'll be able to see at a glance how attractive the market is for you overall, and whether it will help you meet your overall business goals in your desired timeframe.

It's also important to understand that where international expansion is concerned, you're not in full control of everything. Yes, your leadership team is behind the steering wheel, and you can certainly plan your own route, but every country's landscape is different. Getting your business to a good level of penetration in any market can be accelerated, just like you can speed on a highway, but to a great degree you'll be limited by the local terrain, road conditions, and the level of traffic. You have control over some things more than others, and the MARACA model is designed to account for that fact (see Table 5.2).

Let's assume you're a software company based in the United States with ambitions of increasing your presence in Europe. You already have a small number of users, customers, or visitors in Germany, Switzerland, and Sweden, even though you haven't yet been targeting any one of those countries specifically. You'd love to devote some resources to expanding further, such as adding sales headcount focused on one country, but just judging from your own current real-time analytics (RA), they all appear to be similarly attractive (see Table 5.3).

On the MA front, you learn that the economy sizes of Switzerland and Sweden are not the largest the world has to offer, but they're certainly big enough to warrant interest. You estimate that the market for what you're selling is roughly the same in both Sweden and Switzerland, which makes sense given that their GDP size is similar. Germany, however, is one of the biggest European economies, ranking much higher than Switzerland and Sweden, so Germany wins when it comes to MA.

TABLE 5.2. MARACA Components and Level of Control

	Metric	Your Level of Control	Reason
MA	Market availability	Low	The only way the MA can change is if something fundamental about a country's economy changes. Because you have limited control over it, decisions about expansion should never be made based on MA alone.
RA	Real-time analytics	High	Aspects of your business that show up as RA can often readily be improved by employing specific, short-term tactics, such as allocating more resources toward a given country. However, the speed at which those results can be realized and sustained at scale depends largely upon CA. And the decision to allocate resources must also take into account long-term strategy and thus, MA.
CA	Customer addressability	Medium	Here you have some degree of control in how you adapt your business to the reality of each local market. Limited English proficiency might be overcome by localizing your experience. Cultural distance might be overcome by adapting your business model. Economic differences might be overcome by adapting your pricing and packaging. However, some aspects of addressability relate to ease of doing business, government rules, local laws, and cultural issues that you cannot control. For example, in certain new markets, you might need to change your go-to-market model from a direct model to a strategic partnership model, to adapt to those realities.

TABLE 5.3. Hypothetical MARACA Scores by Country

	MA	RA	CA
Germany	High	High	Low
Switzerland	Medium	High	Medium
Sweden	Medium	High	High

Judging from your website traffic data, lead flow, and sales performance, all three countries seem to be doing well and are actually outperforming your domestic market right now. You don't notice any major differences on sales velocity metrics, such as average deal size or sales cycle length. So, the RA is high for all three.

However, when it comes to how well you're doing with CA, the picture looks quite different from one country to the next on a few key fronts:

- **Language.** You don't yet have your product offering or website localized, and while all three markets are English-friendly, you know you can only go so far into Germany without localizing into German. When you look at the percentage of Germans who are comfortable doing business in English only for the high-stakes product you happen to sell, you realize you can only address a fraction of the total available market, or the MA, in Germany today. Sweden has the highest English proficiency of all three.
- **Currency.** It's a tie on this one. You don't offer any currencies other than USD today. You had already been considering adding the Euro to make it easier for companies to pay without having to worry about foreign exchange rates or local tax rates affecting the price they pay in their local currency, or the local customer's total cost to buy your product from their home market.
- **Local presence.** Here, Sweden has another slight advantage. Although you have no employees in any of the three countries, you already have a reselling partner based in Sweden who is eager to do more with you. This partner is strongly encouraging you to

test the waters further by investing a little more in local co-marketing with them.

Which country should you choose? There is no right or wrong answer, without knowing all the details of your business. Your choice will depend on your available budget, your risk tolerance, and how you decide to intensify your efforts. For many companies, I would advise them to go with the "easy" markets first (Sweden in this example) and avoid those that require intensive localization efforts. This can help their company build some basic organizational muscle before trying to lift an international expansion in a more difficult part of the world, one they might find too heavy.

That said, if your plans are big and your company is well-funded, it can sometimes make sense to do the heavier lift, and the more difficult market (Germany in this example), a bit earlier with an eye toward the long term. Organizationally, there is likely to be far more pain up front. But longer term, if your business doesn't break under the weight, it can provide you with some earlier traction in a more difficult market that you can later build on.

In this example, the MARACA framework does not even need to give you a clear answer. Rather, it helps to draw out the differences and force you to think about the choices you can make for your business, in a more explicit and tangible way.

The degree to which you intensify your presence in any market should match the level of risk tolerance you have for your business. Often, the risk tolerance level will map to how well-funded your company is, but it could also map to the stage of market entry you're at, or even the economic situation in your home country or the target countries. In times of recession, you can still expand internationally, but because stakes are higher, your approach will need to be different. Table 5.4 shows some examples of what a company might choose depending on their risk tolerance.

TABLE 5.4. Using MARACA Scores and Risk Levels to Inform Decisions

Risk Tolerance Level	Low	Medium	High
Explanation	You need to be conservative with funding right now and can't afford to invest resources in localization or foreign exchange risks. You also don't want to add salespeople in another country just yet.	You have some budget available to invest, but you don't want to go all in on localization yet, knowing this will require far more resources and a long-term commitment to a new market	You are well-funded, and the economic picture looks stable. Your overall business fundamentals are solid, and you want to start addressing the largest market opportunity available to you, while also addressing medium-sized markets.
Market intensification decision	You decide to lean into your partner's enthusiasm in Sweden for now in order to fine-tune your reselling model. If it works, you can expand it to other countries later.	You opt to hire one salesperson based in Sweden and one in Switzerland. Both markets have a similar size. You'll use this as a learning exercise and pay close attention to differences in performance metrics.	You decide to go all in on Germany, putting together a budget to fund localization of your website, product offering, and core marketing materials. You'll hire a German marketer and build a small sales team with a local leader. Hire one salesperson to focus on Sweden and Switzerland as well.

If you're in the privileged position of having a high risk tolerance, this should mean that you're currently in a supportive macroeconomic business environment and are also well capitalized. You might be somewhat early stage, and have obtained venture capital funding, or perhaps you're already a public company but with a significant bank balance you can use for investments to fuel your growth and keep investors happy.

Most businesses, especially privately owned small and medium-sized businesses (SMBs), fall in the low- and medium-risk categories, even in good economic times. This is why it's important for you to understand that you can go global gradually, and in a more stepwise fashion. In fact, that's the beauty of going global in the digital age. With an online or digital model, international expansion suddenly becomes accessible to every business. The degree of intensification might vary based on how much you can invest in your international growth, but small steps add up, and it's empowering to know you have choices available.

How to Create a More Advanced Country Scorecard

Now that you understand the basics of the MARACA model, you can customize it further, so long as you are using the three dimensions outlined above. Many companies find it helpful to turn the different areas of measurement into numbers, so that they can create a score, or ranking, to help prioritize markets.

For simplicity, I like to use a 10-point scale. This means that each area of the score—MA, RA, and CA—is worth 10 points. If you wish, you can then average them to compute a composite score, though I prefer to leave them separate when the list of potential target countries is manageable, say, anything fewer than eight countries.

Example of a perfect score:
MA/RA/CA = 10/10/10
Composite score = 10

Most markets will never have a perfect score. Very few markets are as "perfect" for us as our home market in terms of customer addressability (CA), and many markets will simply vary due to economy size in terms of market availability (MA). Performance or real-time analytics (RA) is usually going to be best in a company's domestic market, but not always. It depends on which metrics you track. It's very common to see differences in classic metrics like retention that are higher in some markets due to cultural reasons, no matter what type of business you're in. The goal is not for any market to have a perfect score, but rather to use the score to prioritize markets and timing of intensification efforts, as well as to determine appropriate local market strategies.

MA: Market Availability

For MA, one method you can use is to assign 10 possible points, corresponding to either the size of the market in each country (if known) or the number of total target customers in each market.

For example, let's say we are a B2B company based in Canada, and we're selling to SMBs. We can assign size ranges and up to 10 MA points using the SMB count in each country.

SMB Count	Points
4M and up	10
3–3.9M	9
2–2.9M	8
1–1.9M	7
800–999K	6
600–799K	5
400–599K	4
200–399K	3
100–199K	2
Below 100K	1

Our home country of Canada would earn 7 points on this scale, based on the number of SMBs we have in our home market. Yet, a bigger market like the United States would get a 10 in terms of market size, due to it being so large and having so many SMBs. Very few other markets would get such a high rating—for example, perhaps Japan, China, Indonesia, and Nigeria would also rank as a 10 if we're only looking at the raw count of SMBs according to government data sources, which tend to trend alongside population size.

However, you may decide that initially you'll consider only the countries with the most developed economies. This would mean you're only comparing Japan and the United States. In that scenario, you might decide to make certain economy types an explicit omission. Or you could use the estimated total addressable market of each country, which I happen to prefer most of the time over simply things like the number of businesses in each country.

The reason I prefer market size estimates in terms of monetary value is that they are more reflective of opportunity and market share than simply the number of potential customers. The customers already purchasing what you sell is a better gauge of market availability than the number you could theoretically sell to. But not all businesses can get access to that data. Use the best and most reliable data source you can get your hands on.

RA: Real-Time Analytics

The second part of the score is a measure of the traction you're seeing in the market already, largely because of past marketing, sales, and services investments, possibly with spillover effects from markets you already have a stronger presence in. It answers the question, "How are we already doing in this market?"

The cumulative RA score is worth 10 points and is calculated by taking an average of key metrics in each major area of revenue impact as shown in Table 5.5.

TABLE 5.5. Sample Metrics for RA Scoring

Sub-Area	Sample Metrics	What It Tells You
RA—Marketing	Lead flow, traffic	How well is the marketing team delivering for this market?
RA—Sales	Quota attainment, deal size, close rate, sales velocity	How well is the sales term performing here compared to the plan?
RA—Customer success	Retention rate, renewal rate, account growth rate	How well is our customer success team retaining and growing our customer base in this market?

The RA score in aggregate will tell you how you're performing overall in a given country with your existing go-to-market motion. Looking at the funnel breakdown can help you pinpoint specific areas of performance strengths and weaknesses in order to make the necessary adjustments and conduct the necessary deep dives.

You can assign points based on what you would typically consider outstanding performance in any given area, based on what each team or functional leader feels is appropriate, as well as what might be within typical performance ranges for your business. Here are some examples:

RA (Marketing)	Points
100 percent above target	10
75 percent above target	9
50 percent above target	8
25 percent above target	7
10 percent above target	6
Meeting target	5
10 percent below target	4
15 percent below target	3
20 percent below target	2
25 percent below target	1

RA (Sales)	Points
20 percent above target	10
10 percent above target	9
5 percent above target	8
2.5 percent above target	7
Meeting target	6
5 percent below target	5
10 percent below target	4
15 percent below target	3
20 percent below target	2
25 percent below target	1

RA (Customer Success)	Points
10 percent above target	10
6 percent above target	9
2 percent above target	8
Meeting target	7
1 percent below target	6
2 percent below target	5
3 percent below target	4
4 percent below target	3
5 percent below target	2
6 percent below target	1

Now that you have a basic understanding of how the MARACA framework can be used, either to provide a simple high/medium/low snapshot for purposes of country comparison, or a much more detailed scorecard, let's look at how to interpret any MARACA score and apply the results to your business.

First, let's look at how to use CA and MA to make strategy decisions (see Table 5.6). In general, strategy decisions should be made using a combination of CA and MA, leaning toward CA to help determine timing. RA is important too, but generally, you'll want to focus on making improvements in CA, with RA being more of an output to monitor than the core driver of your decisions.

CA: Customer Addressability

This part of the score is a measure of product-market fit and is arguably the most important driver of your company's short- and mid-term strategy decisions. When CA is high, it means lower risk for your business and indicates that you should see results in a shorter time horizon. High CA essentially means a higher and quicker return on your investment in that country.

CA answers the question, "How easily can our product fit into this market?" Your company will have some ability to improve CA,

TABLE 5.6. Using CA and MA to Define International Strategy

CA is . . .	MA is . . .	What to Do
High	Medium to high	Invest early for steady ROI. These markets should yield well in the short and long terms. Push forward, but depending on risk tolerance, create a stepwise approach. You might also target by city or region within the country, to create more momentum. In bigger markets, focus more on boosting addressability score further, especially when it comes to packaging and local market presence.
Medium to high	Low	Consider these markets your low-hanging fruit. Boost the CA score by deepening localization efforts as well as marketing and sales focus. For most markets, there is no need to open a local office in order to achieve full reach. These markets may have less competition from companies with comparable product offerings.
Low	Any	Prioritize countries with high MA within a given region. Boost CA where possible with minimal investment to gain return on original investments but avoid making significant new investments.
Very low	High	Avoid focusing energy on these markets for now. Consider making these markets explicit omissions for now, so that no one in your company mistakenly focuses on them. You might take reactive advantage of incoming opportunities but avoid focusing on these markets aside from perhaps low-risk experiments. Or, where other indicators are strong, or your risk tolerance is very high, focus on boosting CA first to achieve a better product-market fit before you pay close attention to RA.

but the higher the CA from the onset, the less investment required to see ROI.

You should choose your own categories for CA based on the needs of your company and the industry in which you operate, but basically, what you're asking is how difficult it will be to gain market share in a given market, based on the specifics of your business today. This helps you assess how far your company will need to stretch and adapt to fully adjust to the needs of a new market.

Let's assume that for CA, you'll assign 10 possible points, broken down into the following key categories that matter for most businesses:

Economy	20 percent
Packaging and pricing	20 percent
Ease of doing business	20 percent
Language	20 percent
Local market presence	20 percent

The sub-scores are worth 10 points each, weighted evenly and averaged to yield a 10-point score for CA. Here is an at-a-glance view of how you can calculate the scores.

Economy | 10 points possible

High-income = 10
Middle-upper = 7.5
Middle-lower = 5
Lower = 2.5

Pricing and Packaging | 10 points possible

We offer local pricing/packaging that meets the needs of this country = 10
We accept local currency + payments for this country = 5
No customization = 0

Ease of Doing Business Scores | 10 points possible

Top third = 10 points
Middle third = 5 points
Bottom third = 0 points

Language | 10 points possible

Language proficiency level | 4 points possible

> Native = 4 (this country speaks the same language we do)
> High = 3 (this country has high proficiency in our native language)
> Medium = 2 (this country has medium proficiency in our native language)
> Low = 1 (this country has low proficiency in our native language)

Localization | 6 points possible

> High degree of localization required = 6
> Medium degree of localization required = 4
> Low degree of localization required = 2
> Zero localization required = 0

Local presence | 10 points possible

> Country employee presence + many partners = 10
> Country employee presence + some partners = 8
> Regional employee presence + many partners = 6
> Regional employee presence + some partners = 4
> No regional employee presence + many partners = 3
> No regional employee presence + some partners = 2
> No regional employee presence + no partners = 0

It's important to remember that you can get more or less explicit about how many points you give to a certain element based on how you want to weight it. It requires some critical thinking about which pieces of your business will be the hardest to adapt. Ultimately, what you want to take away from your CA scores is a clear sense of how hard it will be to adapt the various areas of your business in a new market.

When thinking about CA, you want to get a basic sense of the following question: How much adaptation will be required for our business overall? This is very different from questions that you'll need to ask later, such as

- How much adaptation will our product require?
- How much will our go-to-market motion require?
- How much will our sales playbook need to adapt?
- Do we need to change our marketing strategy?
- Does our customer service or support offering need to change based on different expectations in this market?

You don't necessarily need to look at all these elements and try to score them all at the outset. For many, you can learn about them in the necessary level of detail only after you've made a commitment to moving into a new market. There is a lot of nuance involved with each of the questions above. You'll need to invest in hiring people on local teams to help you understand exactly how to adapt all these areas of your business. And while you can do some research on these topics, those are not the core questions you have to ask initially when you're assessing which markets to go into. It's fine if you don't have all the answers to these questions yet.

My suggestion is: keep it simple. First focus on the higher-level and big-picture questions that matter most, such as economy type, pricing and packaging, ease of doing business, language, and local presence. These will help you narrow things down, so that you can get to a place where you can answer the deeper questions of how exactly to adapt your business. The more specific decisions of how much to adapt the various parts of your business should be made in partnership with local teams who know the market—and who know your company—with depth.

You should now have a basic understanding of what the model looks like and how it is used in practice. In the chapters that follow, we'll go into more details on how to further develop your MA, RA, and CA, so that you can apply the model to your specific business.

Key Takeaways

- Because every company is unique, there is no one-size-fits-all framework for international expansion. Use any model, including MARACA, mostly as a general guide.
- Keep your focus on countries as early as you can, as opposed to large regions of the world, which are really just groupings of countries. Looking at data too broadly in a region can mask differences and be too generic to be useful.
- Whatever model you use to guide your choices, make sure not only to look just at "how big" and "how easy" a market will be, but also at your internal metrics and initial signs of traction.
- Risk tolerance is an important factor to consider when narrowing down your choices for which markets to scale into.
- When trying to decide between various countries where you have similar traction already, look at MA (market availability) and CA (customer addressability) in combination, to help you narrow down your strategic choices.

6

CALCULATE MARKET AVAILABILITY

If you hope to expand internationally, you will want to know how much opportunity awaits. You'll need a way to quantify the potential and make strategic choices. But how do you size the market when your opportunity is . . . the world? This is a question many business leaders struggle with.

Market availability (MA) is the size of the market within a given country for what your business is selling.

MA is measured in whatever currency you choose, most commonly the currency of the country where you are headquartered, such as US dollars if you're based in the United States.

If you've ever looked into market size for the industry in which your business operates, you've probably noticed a large disparity among different estimates. This is because every group that creates a market size estimate tends to do it in a slightly different way. When I use the term "market availability" (MA), I'm talking about a quantifiable number used to designate the size of opportunity for your business in a given country, no matter what measurement you use.

Many companies want to understand market size, but then aren't really sure what to do with that data once they have it. For that reason, ask yourself the following questions:

- How will this data be used? For what purpose(s)?
- What level of detail is needed to achieve our goals?
- Are global estimates sufficient, or will we need regional and country data?
- How much is spent on our category today with existing competitors?
- How much could potentially be spent on our category in the future?

Your answers to these questions can help inform decisions later on with regard to how to come up with your market sizing estimates.

Temper Enthusiasm for the Largest Markets

Before we discuss market sizing in greater detail, here are some important caveats to keep in mind:

- The biggest market does not always represent the greatest opportunity. The best market opportunity for your company often depends much more on other factors, such as your company's uniqueness, the competition, and the need to adapt (or not) your local offering and current ties to a given market. If you seek a foothold that can give you sustained traction in a given country to drive scale in the long term, these issues often matter far more than the current size of that market.
- A market that's "available" is not always "accessible." Don't confuse market size with your business's ability to actually make a dent in that market. For example, you might enter a market that looks large, only to find that most of that market is already served by a competitor who has locked customers into multiyear contracts with local pricing or some other tailored offering that makes it harder for you to compete.
- A top market today can lose ground to another market tomorrow. For example, newly enacted local laws, which can spring up over

the course of a short time, can make it harder to do business in a given country and might suddenly slow down your growth there. Particularly with technology adoption, dramatic changes can happen within a few years. For that reason, basing your choices on market size alone, in the absence of other factors, can be risky. Remember: market size is changeable, is not something you can control, and is always relative to a specific point in time. Depending on your industry, the local business landscape can change faster than it takes to establish roots and brand awareness for your company in a new market.

In other words, as we discuss market sizing, keep in mind that the biggest market is not always the best, let alone the most important one for your business to focus on at any given point in time.

There are many different ways to size a market, and there are a lot of terms used in the business world that tend to be used interchangeably. In this section, my goal is to break this topic down and make it easier for you to figure out true market availability (MA) for your business.

You've probably heard of total addressable market (TAM), but it's important to understand how TAM breaks down further in order to set realistic goals for your business in any market, whether global, regional, or local. Table 6.1 shows a simple way to think about this generally. It's followed by a hypothetical example.

To make these concepts easier to understand and put some numbers behind them, let's look at a hypothetical example of how we would size the market for a software product that is designed primarily for accounting firms. Let's assume that we have dependable sources showing that the average selling price globally for this type of software, on a subscription basis, is $150 per month, which equates to $1,800 in annual revenue potential from a typical customer. And let's assume that the same sources show that globally, there are a total of 140 thousand accounting firms in our company's domestic market, the United States (see Table 6.2).

TABLE 6.1. Understanding TAM, SAM, and SOM

Market Size Estimate	How to Calculate It	Question to Ask	Time Horizon for Access
TAM Total addressable market	Number of total potential customers × average selling price	How big is the largest possible market for what your company offers?	Long-term
SAM Serviceable addressable market	Number of customers currently able to buy your product × average selling price	For what segment of that market do you have product-market fit?	Mid-term
SOM Serviceable obtainable market	Number of customers served currently by your company and competitors × average selling price	What segment of the market is currently being served with an offering like yours?	Near-term

The concepts that already exist for market sizing are helpful, but things get confusing when we start to slice and dice our data at the country level. Complexity is already inherent in international business planning. You could talk about "country TAM" or "regional SAM" or "nondomestic SOM," but this tends only to add more complexity and can really confuse people.

When talking to others at your company, you'll need a simple way to refer to a local market size outside your domestic market, so that everyone knows what you're referring to. You could call this "country TAM," but if you only talk about the TAM of a country (which is market opportunity you aren't actually able to address yet), you will probably be artificially inflating the market size, which can lead you to set goals that are not realistic.

For that reason, I created the more flexible concept of market availability (MA). My primary goal was to remove complexity and create a universal concept that could be used by any company, no matter which type of market size estimate they might be using, as long as they apply

TABLE 6.2. Using TAM, SAM, and SOM to Calculate Local Market Size

Software for Accounting Firms	Market Sizing Example: United States			
	Question to Ask	Hypothetical Answer	Calculation	Estimate
TAM Total addressable market	How big is the largest possible market for what our company offers?	This includes every single firm, from the smallest to the largest	140 thousand accounting firms that could possibly buy our product in the United States × $1,800	$252 million
SAM Serviceable addressable market	For what segment of that market do we have product-market fit?	Our product isn't mature enough yet for upmarket needs, but can address 80 percent of the market, which are smaller firms	112 thousand accounting firms for which we have good product-market fit × $1,800	$202 million
SOM Serviceable obtainable market	What segment of the market is currently being served with an offering like ours?	We currently have $3M in revenue from our target segment, and we run into 20 key competitors of various sizes. In total, between our customers and theirs, we estimate we serve around 40% of the market today.	56 thousand accounting firms that use us or companies like us today × $1,800	$101 million

it consistently from country to country. Whether it's internally derived or from a third party, or if the calculations used to get to this output come from an estimate you've calculated of TAM, SAM, SOM, or a custom adaptation of these, you can simply call it market availability (MA) when talking about "local market size," which is simpler and easier to remember.

No matter what formula you decide to use to calculate MA, it's important that you focus on a few important principles:

- **Seek data that is trustworthy and reliable, from valid sources.** When possible, leverage existing research from reputable market research firms, such as Gartner, Forrester, IDC, or where available, use data from government research databases. Do not just resort to online search results. Purchase the actual reports if they're available for your industry. If no such external, validated sizing estimates exist, you'll need to come up with your own estimates.

- **Clarify what MA means for your business.** Make your formula as simple and clear as possible, so that everyone can understand how your market size estimates are derived. Before you can make any decisions using this data, your executive team and/or investors need to understand how the figures are calculated. Even if the calculation was done by a third-party firm or government entity, you'll want to be able to explain it clearly and in simple terms.

- **Look for data that is geographically consistent.** You want the data to be as consistent as possible when you compare from country to country. This piece is often the toughest, because when you start digging into market data, you'll find that it can be very difficult to get certain data on a country-by-country basis. Many research firms only offer regional estimates, not country-specific ones. In such cases, you might need to come up with country estimates based on the regional ones.

On this last point, many of the most reliable sources for data are from government sources, but not all governments use standard definitions, not even within the same regions of the world. For example, an SMB in some countries may be any company with 5 to 100 employees, while in others, the definition includes all businesses with 10 to 1,000 employees. Other countries include in their SMB estimates even companies with one employee. A single person can register hundreds of companies in their name, a very common practice in some parts of the world. This could mean that the number of target customers is incredibly misleading, making MA difficult to calculate.

Whenever possible, I encourage you to leverage known market size estimates by respected market research firms. These are created by people who do this for a living and have access to resources such as analysts, algorithms, data sources, and many years of expertise in market sizing that you likely won't have at your company.

The most accurate market size estimates are based on historical data that shows you what was actually spent in a recent time period (such as the prior fiscal or calendar year) on the types of services or products you're selling. Competitor data, if available to you, can also provide a basis for a market size estimate.

However, if you're targeting only a slice of a known and well-sized market, or if you're a category creator with a disruptive technology developing a new market, you'll need to work up your own estimates. Look at the market you're disrupting in order to get a proxy for the size. Even if it's not perfect, it will give you a baseline sense of market opportunity. If you're sizing a market that does not exist yet, estimate what amount your company could obtain from the "old market" and add in an estimate for any net new customers created by your disruptive offering.

There are a few main challenges with coming up with your own estimates:

- Estimating the average selling price (ASP), especially for countries you're not selling into yet
- Estimating the number of potential customers
- Estimating future market growth

Here are a few ways you can come up with an average selling price to include in your MA calculations:

1. **Use real data if you can.** Do you know the ASP of your competitors or your own business in a given country? If not, can you get this data from any public sources? Do you have partners or contacts who might have access to this data?

2. **Do some custom research.** You can survey prospective customers in a given country in order to find out what they would be willing to pay. While this is not necessarily as valid as historical data that tells you what people actually paid, it can be helpful. Third-party research teams can carry out this type of research for you, or you can do it directly if you have the ability to conduct the survey and do the analysis in-house. This data can also be very useful for you to test different price options, packages, and discount levels.

3. **Leverage an indicative metric.** You can map your data to the World Bank's purchasing power parity by country (PPP) metric, or you can use gross domestic product (GDP) per capita. Using PPP is one of the simplest and most effective ways to estimate ASP by country for market sizing purposes. While not always indicative of what people would pay, it's indicative of what they probably should pay based on the reality of their local economy. You can easily find PPP pricing calculators online that enable you to do this.

To provide a simple example of applying an indicative metric to calculate a local ASP, let's assume we're selling a software product in the United States that has an annual subscription price of US$1,000. In this hypothetical scenario, Table 6.3 shows what our ASP might look like in a selection of countries after we adjust for PPP.

It's important to remember that the adjusted price estimates above, which are simply examples and not recommendations, are based on purchasing power parity, which is different from market demand. There are many times when there is a segment of customers who are willing to pay above what is a "fair price" according to purchasing power in a given country, simply because they are outliers within a market, or because of scarcity of your offering in their local market.

However, remember that PPP gives you a good sense of what price will work in order to target the *majority* of customers in a given local market. That is tremendously important when thinking about market availability. The higher your price relative to PPP, the smaller the total number

TABLE 6.3. Using PPP to Estimate ASP by Country

	PPP Adjustment	Local ASP Estimate
Switzerland	131%	$1,306
Israel	117%	$1,173
Denmark	115%	$1,155
Australia	110%	$1,097
Finland	107%	$1,065
Sweden	103%	$1,027
United States	100%	$1,000
Austria	−2%	$985
United Kingdom	−4%	$961
France	−7%	$928
Germany	−8%	$916
Japan	−12%	$878
Singapore	−37%	$631
Chile	−45%	$546
Mexico	−54%	$456
Poland	−56%	$444
Thailand	−61%	$395
Brazil	−64%	$367

of customers you'll have available. The closer you can get to the PPP-adjusted range, the more of the market you'll be able to address.

That said, many companies find that early adopters in new markets will pay a higher price. This lures them into thinking they don't need to adjust their pricing—which is true for a time, but only in the early phase of local market penetration. Just be mindful that keeping your price the same in all markets will ultimately shrink your addressable market and keep you from deepening your company's presence or becoming a leader in the majority of the market.

When thinking about what people are willing to pay in different local markets, never assume that you can charge exactly what your local competitors do, let alone more—unless your offering has something truly special that your customers see value in and that differentiates you from your competitors in that market, and you actually can validate this belief with local feedback from customers in that market.

Local competitors often have better products more tailored to the needs of their local markets in ways you won't even be aware of until later as you grow in that market, so you can't assume these local market leaders will be easy to displace, especially not on their home turf. Most companies tend to over-simplify in this area and apply a single "global ASP" to every country. Doing that can lead to erroneous assumptions about what you can realistically accomplish in a local market.

Customers define the value of your offering differently depending on the country they're in. If you can't easily adapt your product, consider adapting your pricing and packaging.

For that reason, I strongly suggest complementing any third-party estimates you obtain or data you calculate yourself with data you collect from actual customers in local markets, or from local competitors, to truly understand what price they will be willing to pay for your product. This may not be the same price they're willing to pay for a competitor's product that better meets their needs. Keep in mind that as your offerings evolve, you'll need to keep doing this, because the local market itself will change, as will your local competition.

If possible, before you start selling in a given market, find some customers to try or test out your product for free and give you feedback. Then ask them two key things: (1) where they see the value in your product, and (2) what they would pay for your product, compared to what they currently pay for similar products from your competitors. This might be the most valuable research you do when you're trying to figure out the true potential of any local market, saving you a tremendous headache later. If you stumble into a market without this information, you will only have a sense of local TAM, but you won't have any clear idea of your local SAM, let alone your local SOM. It's important to know that long before you start hiring salespeople, making investments in marketing, and committing in bigger ways.

Discounting Can't Replace Local Pricing and Packaging

You might be tempted to go for simply using one price, in one currency, for all countries in the world. This can work for some situations but can come with significant disadvantages. Essentially, if you fail to customize your offering in a local market, you often run the risk of throwing the problem over to your salespeople, making them less productive and less enabled to hit their targets. This means that instead of empowering your salespeople to sell, you are burdening them with micro-level market research, one deal at a time, negotiating discounts in each country, and then analyzing the data after the fact. Why not just talk to local customers ahead of time instead, to save your company all this trouble?

Sometimes, companies are growing so fast that they don't take a moment to stop and think about what might happen if they took a chance to pause and reassess instead of driving too furiously into a new market with the known of their original pricing and packaging strategy.

If you're a company that processes large volumes of smaller deals, and you largely sell with a digital go-to-market motion that is highly scalable and easy to take global, keeping things in one price early on might seem like the simplest way to collect data on what the market is willing to pay initially, but keep in mind that you could be alienating a good percentage of the market and creating a perception of your brand that might not be what you want to project in the long term, if you completely miss the target on getting your local pricing right.

Why does this matter? If you price yourself too high, you can cast yourself as an upmarket competitor in a given country, where you're really intending to be seen as a midmarket player globally. If all your branding, messaging, and positioning is really for a customer profile in one segment of the market, but how you come across in some markets is different due to the economy being a mismatch, your marketing efforts simply won't be as effective, and you'll only be able to target a certain percentage of the local market you wish to penetrate.

So, what should you do about it? Even if you already have some initial traction in a new market, you should seek to understand two key things. First, what aspects of your offering do customers in each country actually value most? This isn't so hard to find out. Survey them, or talk to them, and find out what parts of your product or service and overall offering appeal to them most. Ask them to rank these aspects, so you can easily spot differences by country. Then, once you know what they value, ask yourself if your pricing and packaging map to the things they value.

For example, say your company is selling a software product with implementation services in your home market of Sweden. In most Nordic countries, where the population is small and the cost of human labor is high, people are glad to pay for automation and for outsourcing of services. You may create a package that includes your software along with implementation services that is very popular in not only Sweden but in other, similar developed economies.

But let's say you're seeing demand in an Eastern European country like Poland, where the population happens to be large and highly tech savvy, and the cost of labor is much lower. Perhaps customers in Poland are happy to pay the same price for software, but not for services, because they'll see this as an inflated cost compared to what they could achieve locally in their market by doing things themselves. For this reason, you truly need to understand what your customers see as value before you take a pricing and packaging strategy that works in one country (or even several) and apply it elsewhere in the world. If you discount too much, you risk actually losing business or devaluing the service in the eyes of customers in your new market. So, pricing and packaging is an important area of focus for companies as they go global, and not one that should be treated lightly.

Another common phenomenon companies encounter is that, initially, they don't need to discount in a new local market, because demand for what they are selling is high, and they are largely reaching early adopters who are more likely to take risks and embrace new technologies in spite of what the majority of the market might perceive to be too expensive. In other words, a company might see great traction in a local market in the beginning without even needing to discount. It's when a company gets deeper into a local market that they begin to truly understand the needs of the majority of customers they are targeting, and this is actually when the need for adaptation is even greater than it is in the early phases of local market penetration.

In other words, initial market entry might be easier when it comes to pricing and packaging, needing limited adaptation at first, but market intensification can be more painful because this is when more adaptation is required to deepen your presence in a new market.

How to Estimate Prospective Customer Count by Country

Now that you have an estimated ASP by country, you'll need a customer count to multiply it by in order to come up with an estimate for MA, market availability, or market size by country. There are several ways you can estimate the number of customers available in a given market.

- **Government sources with industry data.** You can usually find customer counts using industry data, broken down by size range via government sources for the country in question. Countries like Canada, Mexico, and the United States use the North American

Industry Classification Codes (NAICS). This enables a high level of comparability between these three countries. The European Union uses a similar concept called Nomenclature of Economic Activities (NACE). This makes it easier to compare from one European country to the next, although some countries adopt this more strictly than others. Some national governments additionally use their own separate classifications that may or may not perfectly map to NACE.

- **Estimates from market research firms.** Many market research firms often do this type of homework for other studies they are working on, so you can ask them for estimates of customer counts for the countries you're interested in, using the typical profile of your target customer. You can also commission a market research firm to come up with estimates for you using criteria you specify.

- **Estimates based on competitor data.** If you know from credible sources such as public filings that a competitor has a given amount of revenue coming from a particular market, and you know their market penetration, you can apply your local ASP to come up with an estimated customer count by country. This can be particularly helpful when there is ample data available from a public company or category leader. For example, if your competitor has revenue of US$1 million coming from Germany, and their average deal size is US$1,000, you can estimate that they have around a thousand customers there. Let's assume they have a 10 percent share of the market. This means the total number of customers you can target in the German market is approximately 10 thousand. You can apply the same logic to each country for which you have estimates available from competitors to come up with a rough customer count.

- **Estimates based on aligned metrics.** Let's say you're selling an online service to consumers that requires internet access. You can take the total number of consumers in that country and apply an aligned metric, such as a country's level of internet penetration, and apply it to each market to get a more realistic sense of how many consumers are actually available to you. For example, if you are a business-to-consumer company targeting customers in the United States, where internet penetration is 91 percent, you can assume a higher percentage of available market in Canada (where internet penetration is 97 percent) or in the United Kingdom (where it's 95 percent) or a lower percentage in Mexico, where it's 73 percent.

- **Reverse-engineered estimates.** If you already have local market size estimates, even from different sources, you can divide that market size estimate by the ASP in order to get a rough customer count. For example, if the market for what you're selling is estimated to be US$500 million in Germany and US$450 million in France according to other sources, divide these numbers by the local ASP you came up with in the prior step (see Table 6.4).

You might not necessarily need a customer count estimate if you already have a market size estimate for a given country, but I recommend coming up with one, because as you are planning, you'll typically revert back to these figures again and again. As the market changes (and as ASP changes), and as you collect more data about a given country, you can refer back to the customer count number and update it as well.

Once you have some basics like customer count and local market size estimates, you can look for data on how fast the market is growing and apply the growth rate to the market size to understand how fast it's growing. Your best bets for obtaining this information are:

TABLE 6.4. Applying ASP Country Estimates to Compute Market Size

Country	Market Size Estimate	ASP Estimate	Customer Count Estimate
France	$450M	$928	484,914
Germany	$500M	$916	545,852

- **Local government sources for the industry you're selling into.** Find out how much your industry is projected to grow year over year, or how much it grew in previous years.
- **Data from market research firms.** Often, market research firms will have estimates for local market growth or can help estimate these for you.
- **Competitor data.** This can be especially useful if you have year-over-year growth figures for the category leader and a sense of the geographic revenue split. You can also take a look at public information on local competitors. In many countries, especially European ones, this data is openly available via government portals, even for private companies. Take an average of the growth rate for top competitors in each market to get a sense of how your market size is growing in each country.
- **End-customer growth rates.** Is the end customer's market growing at a known rate? If so, sometimes you can piggyback off this information. Look for reports that have growth rates for either your target persona or future compound annual growth rates (CAGR), such as, "The # of chief security officers increased by 12 percent in 2023 . . ." or "The offline ads market has a projected CAGR of 38 percent over the next three years . . ."

You can also look at GDP growth for each country as a proxy if you cannot find any other useful data by country. However, I would caution that this is usually too generic to be useful. When possible, use actual data, such as competitor data, even if you only have a small sample size to work with. This is usually far more relevant, as it's indicative of the exact space you are in, whereas the general trend in any economy is an aggregate and won't be as helpful to you.

To avoid creating too much confusion or complexity, keep in mind that you don't need to find data at this level for every single country in the world, even if you currently sell into more than a hundred countries. It's more important to focus your efforts on a smaller number of countries than to attempt to be comprehensive. When you're doing this type of analysis, I recommend you try to keep your number of target countries to no more than 10.

For purposes of MA, pick the countries that make the most sense for your business—these will usually be the ones with the largest economies, ones where your industry is known to have a solid presence, or ones that your competitors are known to succeed in—and focus on those. If there are outliers where your company is seeing traction, we'll cover that in the real-time analytics (RA) stage. Or, if you pick countries with appealing MA that are too difficult to address, you'll find that out later when we get to customer addressability (CA).

GOSTUDENT CASE STUDY
High-Speed International Growth

GoStudent, a top European ed-tech platform founded in 2016, is currently valued at €3 billion. Within the space of less than two years during the pandemic, the company went from operating primarily within their home country of Austria and neighboring Germany to having a presence in 20 different markets in Europe and the Americas. Today, 70 percent of the company's net new customers come from outside their home market. How did they go global with such impressive speed?

It started with their investors highlighting international expansion as a top priority. As Chief Growth Officer Laura Warnier explains, "Our investors told us we needed to prove success outside our core market in order to achieve true unicorn status." And so, Warnier sprung to action, leading the company in its expansion efforts, first launching in France in August 2020, followed by 15 markets in quick succession in 2021.

There were several reasons for choosing France first. "We looked at the private education sector in Europe and saw that France had the highest level of spending," Warnier explains. "It was a culture that we knew, with the same time zone, and we could easily travel there even during COVID." It was also a market in which Warnier, a Belgian, herself spoke the language natively. "It's always easier to expand internationally in a country where you know the market and language, so we said, let's try it out in France."

However, Warnier believes that many companies tend to overthink their market selection efforts in the beginning, even when they are choosing between markets that are actually quite similar. "There is a risk if you spend too much time doing market assessments that you'll never dare to actually go," she asserts. "You can come up with the same number of pros and cons no matter which market you choose." For GoStudent, the process was to first focus on any markets that would be stated omissions, coming up with a list of markets with red flags. Warnier suggests asking, "Are there any markets where it's going to be difficult to do business, due to laws in place there related to what you're selling, or some other significant barrier?" If so, she advises taking those off the list to narrow it down.

Once you have chosen a country, the focus needs to be on execution. "Focus on how, not if," Warnier advises. "After you commit, have confidence in the fact that you're going there, it's a learning process, and you will figure it out." For GoStudent, rapid acceleration into many markets meant prioritizing two key things: (1) creating a repeatable playbook with a cross-functional team and (2) hiring for culture fit.

"After our launch into France, I hired a project manager who took notes of every step, what needed to be done for HR, finance, legal, and so on, so that we could use it as a project management tool for future launches. This enabled us to know for the next launch how to sequence

(*continued*)

(*Continued*)

each step, and where dependencies would be," explains Warnier. "That playbook enabled us to launch in 15 new countries in just one year."

The organizational learning that international expansion entailed also meant having people involved in the launch process from every key area of the business. "In some cases, a function needed a dedicated person for the launch, but in others, they needed to spend only 10 percent of their time on launch activities," Warnier notes. "What we did for each market was to hire a founding team of four people—sales, marketing, customer success, and tutor recruitment. We always hired people who fit our culture globally, but who also knew the local culture deeply."

Getting culture fit right is hugely important when launching in any new market, not only because these are the seeds your company will grow from in each country, but because those early team members will be the ones to help adapt your local strategy as time goes on. "In the beginning, your playbook is usually 80 percent global and 20 percent local," explains Warnier. "Over time, you'll naturally move away from a global strategy to a much more local strategy, but you cannot do that from the very beginning."

One critical thing that GoStudent found helpful to drive long-term success in each market was vetting the founding team members for each market thoroughly to ensure confidence in those early hiring decisions. But once you've hired them, you need to give them the right level of autonomy to do what is best for their markets. "You can't have speed without trust," Warnier points out. Indeed, GoStudent's rapid international expansion would not have been possible without trust—in both the repeatability of their playbook and in their ability to hire for culture fit. This, combined with confidence in their ability to adapt and learn while executing, are two major reasons for GoStudent's rapid rise to global success.[1]

Key Takeaways

- Resist the understandable urge to leap straight into the largest market you find. Some markets require your business to adapt more than others, and could distract your company, compromising the focus you need to achieve other business goals.
- Clarify what you really mean when using terms like "TAM" and "market size." Be clear on whether you're talking about opportunity in a specific country, a region, or in your total global market.
- If you don't have exact pricing data for each local market, you can approximate it by using aligned metrics like gross domestic product (GDP) per capita and purchasing power parity (PPP).
- Be leery of using discounting as a replacement for local pricing and packaging because this can create a sense of your brand in other markets that ends up being different than what you actually want to convey. This can be very difficult to change later.
- Remember not to overcomplicate your earliest market selections and instead focus on how you will execute, as GoStudent did. Your company will naturally adapt and learn as you go.

7

PICK YOUR REAL-TIME ANALYTICS

Companies today have access to more data than ever. From dashboards in marketing automation and CRM tools and reports in sales enablement software to data from conversion optimization tools, there is no shortage of information with which to make international expansion decisions. These analytics also have the advantage of being available in real time, which is essential for businesses that have monthly, weekly, or even daily sales targets to hit.

Most businesses with a digital model use a set of real-time analytics referred to as "funnel metrics," or what today are more commonly known as "flywheel metrics" to represent the various stages of a customer journey or lifecycle. The notion of a flywheel is more appropriate in the digital age, because of its highly continuous nature. It's also the perfect way of illustrating why, if you want to put your local customers at the center of your thinking, you'll need to view the various stages of their interactions with your company not as static phases a customer "passes through," but as a more ongoing and continuous motion.

These metrics usually look at a few key areas:

- Attract (marketing). How well are you attracting prospects to your website?

- Engage (sales). How well are you converting those prospects into leads and then into customers?
- Delight (customer success). How well are you retaining those customers and converting them into promoters of your brand?

Table 7.1 lists some sample categories of metrics in each of these major areas. Beneath each category of metrics, there are usually many different pieces to look at. For example, many companies hire analysts just to focus on one area, such as website analytics. At larger companies, entire teams exist, usually within revenue operations, for the purpose of looking at all these data sources. It's not uncommon for companies to monitor hundreds, if not thousands, of different metrics.

In theory, having access to so much data is great. Each metric completes one piece of the puzzle to tell us how a company is performing and what decisions we should make. The problem is that when we look at this data through an international lens and try to compare data from one country to another, the numbers can be misleading, especially when looked at in isolation from a company's broader strategy. These numbers can easily distort your perception of a given country, giving you the impression that a market will be either easier or harder for your company to succeed in than it might really be.

Ideally, you should choose only the top metrics in every area, and no more than three or four metrics per function. For example, Table 7.2 shows what a simple RA scorecard might look like.

TABLE 7.1. Sample Flywheel Metrics to Track by Country

Sample Flywheel Metrics to Track for Each Focus Country		
Attract	Engage	Delight
Brand awareness	Conversion rates	Retention rates
Social reach	Lead flow	Cross-sell / upsell
Traffic data	Sales cycle length	Account growth
Website analytics	Average deal size	Customer satisfaction scores
		Net promoter scores

TABLE 7.2. Example of a Simplified RA Scorecard

	Country A	Country B	Country C
Traffic (monthly visitors)	15,000	8,000	4,000
Lead flow (monthly, per sales rep)	50	30	20
Lead to customer conversion rate (close rate)	4%	3%	5%
Sales cycle length (days)	30	20	10
Average selling price	$10,000	$8,000	$12,000
Customer retention	95%	90%	85%
Customer satisfaction score	75%	70%	80%
Net promoter score	7	6	8

In this example, you'll notice that some countries have positive performance in some areas but score worse in others. This is a typical scenario. It's less important to watch how they compare to one another than how these trends change over time, and to work to improve the most critical metrics that are most closely tied to your company's strategic goals.

Keep your North Star metrics to a minimum when you're expanding in multiple local markets at once. Multiply the number of metrics you track today by the number of countries you plan to focus on, to get a sense of how complex this can become as your business grows.

Avoid Misinterpreting Marketing Signals as Market Potential

One common pitfall is when companies make decisions about country strategy by using data from just one area of their flywheel. Because marketing is the first in line to capture data from different countries and do early market research, it's also usually the function that carries a huge responsibility in this area.

One challenge many companies run into when using their real-time analytics (RA) is that they jump to conclusions about a market based on some promising signs when they're early in a market with limited experience there. They assume that they have a high chance of success in a new market when they see promising signals, just because they might have had success in their home market when they saw similarly promising signals.

Let's say you're a US-based company's chief marketing officer (CMO) who is reviewing a report of your website traffic. For many years, 80 percent or more of your traffic has come from the United States. However, you notice that a larger percentage of your traffic is now coming from India. This might tempt you to hire a marketer to focus specifically on India, so that you can better figure out how to convert that traffic into leads.

You do some basic market research and learn that India appears to have a huge potential market for your products or services. Let's assume that you have a sales team that can cover that time zone. It seems logical that you would want to leverage your success with obtaining traffic from India and allow this to inform your international strategy.

Unfortunately, this is a classic example of a "market pull" metric that can mislead a company into making investments that won't yield results as easily as one might think. The CMO will need to work with others at the company and think through the following questions before pursuing an India strategy:

- **What are the reasons we're seeing such high traffic from India?** India has an enormous population. It's possible that it's because the company has website content available that is attracting large numbers of visitors from India, many of whom speak English, even if they are not directly interested in what the company is selling.
- **Do our sales metrics tell a similar story in India?** Often, sales metrics are where you'll notice major disparities by market, especially if you adopt identical pricing for emerging and developed markets. If you're a US-based company and haven't adjusted your

pricing strategy for India, it will be very difficult to succeed there. Typical examples of metrics where you'll see trouble are an increased sales cycle duration (it usually takes longer to close deals in markets where the value isn't as obvious) and a lower average selling price.

- **Do our retention metrics also look good in India?** It's important not to stop just at the sales metrics, and to look at the full customer life cycle. If your customers don't stay with you for very long and tend to churn out quickly, or if they fail to upgrade or otherwise follow your ideal path for account growth, it's a sign that you're not ready for that market.

- **Do we actually deliver the same value to customers in India?** Ultimately, if your sales metrics don't look good in a given market, it's not usually the fault of the sales team in question. It's often due to a mismatch between the customer's perception of value and the company's product offering. Either it's priced too high for that market, or what's included isn't completely relevant for the local customer, or both. Getting your product offering right is the single most important factor for success in a new market. Yet, it's usually the one companies leave until last.

Another common pitfall companies face is that they ignore signals from a given market, especially if the market isn't one of the largest global economies that tends to attract attention. They might chalk up certain performance metrics to simply a good sales team, failing to see that all the signs of a ripe market opportunity are in front of them.

Let's say you're a sales leader in Europe with a team that covers many markets and a small subteam focused on the Nordic market. You notice that your direct sales team, as well as your channel sales team, both seem to have great success in Finland. The average selling price (ASP) is 20 percent higher there than in any other European countries where you're selling. The sales cycle is also shorter on average. And your lead-to-deal conversion rate is nearly double there compared with other European countries.

You keep adding sales hires for the Nordics overall, but you assume the Finland factor must be a fluke. After all, Sweden is a bigger market. You don't want to put all your eggs in one basket, and you need to keep the territories balanced to avoid friction on the team. Rather than lean too heavily into Finland and get your team to focus there exclusively, you spread your sales team across all the Nordic countries instead. What are the problems with this approach?

- **Less effective marketing campaigns.** If the sales team continues to spread their team across many countries, the job of the marketing team becomes far more difficult. It's far easier to create targeted campaigns by country than to target too many countries at once.
- **Slower local gains in all markets.** The diluted marketing approach, as opposed to a focused one, means that the company will be slower to make significant gains in terms of brand awareness, word of mouth, and obtaining local case studies.
- **Lower revenue contribution.** Instead of wasting their time on countries with a lower ASP, the sales team could be contributing significantly more (20 percent) every quarter to the company's top-line revenue.
- **Decreased collaboration and training.** The sales team could be sharing their learnings with each other about competition in one market, instead of developing knowledge silos within the team that will necessarily be diluted across multiple markets.

Of course, the bigger problem in this example is that the sales leader in question is making decisions that determine international strategy without anyone else in the company realizing it. For this reason, international strategy needs to be explicit. Otherwise, it's easy to see how various parts of a company can "go rogue" and make their own decisions that can have long-term consequences.

Keep Metrics Country-Focused

Business leaders can easily forget when defining their real-time analytics that these need to start at the strategy level. Data becomes difficult to trust when you have too many mixed variables. In an effort to simplify, you might be tempted to lump many countries together into a single regional grouping for purposes of data analysis. What this really means is that you have a regional strategy, but no local country strategy. For example, the commonly used term "EMEA" (Europe, Middle East, and Africa) consists of all of the countries spread across three continents. It's usually a huge warning sign when a company has an EMEA team, but no prioritization in place for which countries in EMEA should be the primary focus, and thus, get most of the resources available for investment.

One common area of pushback, and a legitimate reason why companies don't like to focus on countries too early in their journey, is that they find the data to be overwhelming. But this is usually because they are focused on too many countries at a time, doing a "peanut butter spread" across an entire region. It's not the fact that they can view the data by country that overwhelms them. It's the idea that they need to look at data from so many countries simultaneously.

This is another reason why focus and clarity are hugely important for international expansion. Focus on fewer countries initially. Develop a playbook for those, and then apply that playbook to similar countries with adjustments. If you try to apply your domestic market playbook to all countries simultaneously, you'll end up spreading your company and its resources way too thin. Then, your real-time analytics (RA) won't be useful, because any metrics you look at regionally are too broad and will conceal important local trends.

Set Different Targets for Different Markets

One very real challenge companies face with RA is figuring out what their performance targets should be for individual countries. It's incredibly important that you not try to manage an entire country's business in the same way you manage your domestic market business, or that you try to apply sweeping global targets uniformly across geographies that behave very differently.

Don't use your domestic market performance to set targets for other markets. Markets are different, and where your company is within them will vary too.

Let's take a classic example: sales cycle length in Japan versus the United States, for B2B companies. In a culture like the United States, autonomy and individualism are prioritized, both in society at large but also in business settings. Therefore, decision-making is usually entrusted to a small number of people in B2B transactions, and deals can happen very quickly. Let's say your sales cycle length in the United States is 20 business days.

You apply the same sales process in Japan, but your sales cycle length is now 60 days instead of 20. You wonder why the sales team can't make it happen as quickly as your US team, assuming perhaps that they are less experienced, or don't perform as well. What's really happening, in most cases, is that the environment is simply different. In societies that are more collectivist in nature, the business impact is that deals take longer, because more individuals need to get on board with the decision to begin with.

However, on the flip side, most companies with a B2B product offering, no matter what industry they are in, find Japanese customers to be the most loyal of those in any country, boasting the highest retention rates. A US-based company doesn't look at those numbers and think, "Now, why isn't the US team keeping up? They had better get their act together."

Instead, they tend to look at the retention rates for Japan and think, "Well, isn't that interesting," or "Isn't that nice." But the same cultural attribute of Japanese society that makes the sales cycle longer is the one that makes the retention better. It's a culture where relationships take longer to build, but also are viewed with an assumption they're going to last.

From a Japanese customer perspective, once they commit to a relationship, it would be culturally taboo to simply break that relationship abruptly out of nowhere. It would be disrespectful and inconsiderate. There is so much more consideration that has to happen up front to decide whether a Japanese customer—and all of their colleagues in a B2B setting—are willing to make such a big and important commitment. Through the American lens, loyalty isn't a big deal, and the stakes are much lower. If the relationship is no longer of value, there is no cultural shame in ending it and moving on. Thus, the risk is lower up front, and the sales cycle will tend to be shorter.

If you always use your home market as the gold standard to compare other markets to, you might be overlooking opportunities in markets where you are actually likely to outperform your domestic market. So, what does this mean in terms of setting targets for your company? You should first figure out your country benchmarks, then find ways to improve them. This is very different from operating from a baseline assumption that your global average or domestic setpoint should inform what you can achieve in other places.

Seek incremental improvement in each and every market, as opposed to being overly tied to hitting a specific target that might not be relevant for certain countries.

As a general guide, the more collectivist a society, the longer the sales cycle tends to be, and the better the retention tends to be. The more individualistic a society, the harder retention can be to achieve, and the shorter the sales cycle usually will be. Of course, retention is also driven by product-market fit in a market, so you can't make broad assumptions about why certain things are happening, and of course you want to avoid generalizing about an entire country. At the same time, it's important to be aware that cultural differences really do drive the relationships between your company and your customers.

When setting local targets, it can also be useful to look back at the data from earlier on in your journey in your home market. For example, if a few years ago, your average selling price (ASP) was lower and it has gradually increased over time, you might see a similar trend in each new market you enter. I recommend mapping your key metrics over time to look at the trend, then figuring out what your trajectory will be in each new market if it follows the same general trend. Did you see a year-over-year revenue increase of 25 percent in Year One, with a slowdown by Year Five? If so, you might plan for a similar deceleration in each new market you enter.

The reason time in the market matters so much is really related to brand maturity. If you're an unproven brand in a local market, you can expect it to be harder to sell to customers when they don't even know your brand, let alone trust you. It takes time to build a strong local brand, so you can't assume that your metrics will look the same in each part of the world. Don't assume that your brand in your home market will have much leverage in a new market, because usually you have to build a brand in each market locally from scratch with minimal if any halo effect from other markets.

Net Promoter Score: Should You Use It Globally?

Many companies use the net promoter score (NPS) methodology to measure their overall performance and customer happiness. This can be a very useful tool for local markets, but with a few caveats:

- **Sample size matters.** Generally, unless you can get responses from 50-plus customers in each market, you shouldn't even bother looking at the data, as it won't have much validity.

- **Don't use NPS too early.** Sometimes, companies get wedded to looking at NPS data and forget the importance of talking to customers. If you start looking at NPS too early in your journey in each country, before you truly understand the unique needs of each local market, the data simply won't give you the true story.
- **Recognize regional differences.** Most US-based companies will see certain markets rate them much more highly (Latin America, for example) while others rate much more conservatively (Japan is notorious for this). This doesn't always mean that your company is doing that much better or worse in those markets. In part, it's usually because different cultures tend to have different rating scales to begin with.
- **Keep an eye on the trends instead of using raw scores.** Avoid setting a raw NPS score as a target for all markets. Instead, if you must apply a single target globally, aim to increase your scores by a certain percentage across all markets.
- **Don't compare too strictly with your current home market scores.** You've been operating in your domestic market the longest. It's unfair to presume that you'll perform as well in markets where your company has less experience. Keep an eye on the long-term view, and what your NPS was in the early days of entering your home market, as a basis for comparison with new countries.

Now that you've identified the top metrics that matter, and you've calculated what these look like for each major country, you can monitor progress and make adjustments to boost your performance in each market. To do that, you'll need a clear cadence for communicating these key metrics to the right people at your company. Typically, this will include a combination of executives for each go-to-market function (marketing, sales, customer success) and your regional leaders within core functions, as well as your partners in Finance. You can use a monthly or quarterly international steering group meeting to review these key performance metrics and keep your business on track. It also helps to set up a dashboard with these key metrics that you can send out on a recurring basis to keep these metrics top of mind for regional teams.

Key Takeaways

- Make sure to keep your core flywheel metrics aligned with your business strategy, and don't pick too many things to monitor lest it become overwhelming when you cut the data by country.
- Avoid setting the same targets for every country, recognizing that your business is likely at a different phase of penetration in each market.
- Strive for incremental improvement on the specific metrics that matter and roll up to your north star metrics (LTV, CAC, net new revenue growth, etc.) The second-layer metrics that can move the needle the most on the higher-level business metrics are sometimes different from one country to another.
- If you use net promoter score (NPS), make sure to take into account differences in how people interpret the scale in different cultures. Consider using a more universal metric, such as customer satisfaction (CSAT) either in addition to or instead of NPS.

8

MEASURE CUSTOMER ADDRESSABILITY

Now, let's explore the final and most complex area of the MARACA model, customer addressability (CA). While I say this area is complex, it's because understanding your product-market fit in a new local market is not something that can always be done with clear and simple numbers.

For market availability (MA), you really only need one column in a spreadsheet to indicate a quantifiable market size, and as many rows as you have countries you want to compare. For real-time analytics (RA), most companies only have a few top-line key performance indicators to measure traction in a given market, so let's say three more columns. CA is much, much harder to plot into a system that enables you to objectively compare one market to another.

When I ran this model and did a CA exercise for the very first time, I needed 12 separate columns for the CA section. Because the company was already operating in many markets, my analysis included all 130 countries deemed of economic importance by the World Bank. This yielded 1,560 distinct data points for CA alone. That's why CA is so much harder to calculate than MA and RA. Most companies won't need to go to this level of rigor, especially if they're only comparing a small number of countries. While your CA computation can become this nuanced, it doesn't have to be. It can be as simple or as complex as you need it to be. Let's walk through some examples to make CA easier to understand.

The Basics of Local Customer Addressability

At the highest level, the bigger the gap in culture and language between the country your business knows best (usually your home market) and the one you are targeting for local intensification, the harder it will be for your company to understand the needs of, develop empathy for, and properly address your customers in a given local market. But these are not the only things that matter when it comes to determining your ability to truly address the needs of your local customers.

For example, barriers to payment are some of the highest risk barriers you need to surpass, because if you don't, potential customers will abandon you during the checkout process or upon signing a contract, simply because (even though you did a great job getting them to the final stage) you failed to meet their needs at a critical moment: when it's time to pay.

One quote I often refer to when measuring the importance of local payments is from Renato Beninatto, chairman and co-founder of Nimdzi Insights: "The closer you get to a customer's wallet, the more important localization becomes." This holds true for all companies going global, but especially once they get past the early adopter phase in any new local market.

With localization, most people first think about language and translation, and those factors are definitely important. But as you go deeper into new markets, *country-specific adaptations* often matter even more than linguistic ones do, especially if they come into play at the time of payment. Make sure you offer both the right currency and the right payment types for your local markets, or all the other work you did to adapt your local go-to-market motion to get the customer to that point might be in vain.

Beyond the obvious things like payment types and currency, and especially if you're selling to business buyers, consider things like billing and collections processes, account renewal cadence, and even automated notifications, and how these might need to vary slightly from one country to another to achieve maximum impact. Often, there is low-hanging fruit in all these areas that doesn't require a heavy lift but can have a significant impact on how your customers perceive you when it comes time to pay for your products and services.

NETFLIX CASE STUDY
Focus on Low-Barrier Markets First

What happens if you prioritize the markets with the lowest barriers to entry as you're expanding internationally, adding more complicated markets later on? One example we can look to is Netflix. Headquartered in the United States, the company began offering a streaming-only option in the United States and Canada in 2010, expanding into Latin America in 2011, and into the United Kingdom, Ireland, and Nordic markets in 2012. By 2017, the streaming service went from being available in just a small number of countries to 190 countries, a path that has been dubbed "exponential globalization" by Trinity College professor Louis Brenann in his article in *Harvard Business Review*.[1]

When you're thinking about real-time analytics (RA), it's important to consider not only your own company's growth targets, but also, the competitive environment you're in, and the local barriers that may stand in your way to achieving those targets. Which markets will help you reach those goals the fastest? Netflix is rather unique in its international expansion choices for several reasons. Competition from both local and global purveyors of video content is high. Also, the barriers for competing in local markets can be high too. Netflix must secure deals for new content one region or country at a time. The company also has to comply with local laws and regulations about what type of content can be made available and in which ways.

What is interesting about Netflix's international growth strategy is that it is one of the few US-based companies that focused on intensifying in the least challenging markets first. When the bar to entering a new market is higher (due to regulations or other reasons), this becomes more important. Netflix chose to target the adjacent market of Canada first, building its international muscle along the way. After that, the company looked at factors such as broadband internet access, availability of customers who could afford the service, and market similarities.

In the more recent waves of international expansion, Netflix added many languages, focused on building strong local partnerships, improved its mobile offerings, and deepened its knowledge of many local markets. Today, the company develops original content, often by local creators for local markets, but also brings local stories to global markets as well, reaping the benefits of its highly global presence, thanks to its multiphased expansion strategy along the way. Per its financial results for Q3 2022, Netflix has roughly 32 percent of its subscribers based in the United States and Canada, with the remaining 68 percent in other parts of the world, making its global footprint a key differentiator from its competitors.[2]

Key Questions to Ask When Calculating CA

How your company calculates CA will vary depending on the specifics of your business. When you come up with your customized CA calculation, you might want to consider including some of the items listed in Table 8.1, spanning several key categories.

You don't have to include all these items. For example, early-stage companies, or those that have decided to go remote-first from day one, might choose to eliminate the question about whether they have an office in a given country, as it would not apply. Whatever items you decide to include, you can rank on a scale from 1 to 10. You can also weight these

TABLE 8.1. Key Questions to Help Determine CA Metrics

Category	Sub-Category	Question to Ask
Payment	Currency	Do we offer the currency of the local market?
	Payment type	Do we support the most common payment types of the local market?
Product	Pricing	Do we offer pricing that was developed with this market in mind?
	Packaging	Do we offer any packaging or bundling that was tailored based on this market's unique needs?
Language	Proficiency	What percentage of people in the local market speak the home market language that we already support?
	Degree of localization	To what degree have we localized the experience for the local market?
Presence	Employees	Do we have employees who live in this market?
	Office	Do we have a physical office facility in this market?
	Partners	Do we have partners or resellers in this market?
Operations	Type	What is the level of economic development?
	Ease	How does the country rank for ease of doing business?

scores, ranking certain aspects higher than others. Let's look at an example to understand it better.

Let's assume we're leading a software company based in the United States that is seeing strong RA scores in all the Nordic countries, a common scenario given that Nordic countries tend to be some of the earliest adopters of tech products. Customers in these countries are especially receptive to companies selling in English because English is a standard part of their education systems.

We want to expand our presence in these new markets by hiring a local salesperson, but based on our MA scores, the markets seem to be equally attractive. We only have the budget to hire one headcount for now. Where should we hire them? And how can the CA score help us better understand which country to choose?

Since we have a presence in France and Germany, our business already accepts payment in Euros. However, we do not yet accept Swedish Krona. When we look at both Sweden and Finland side by side, the markets appear nearly the same in terms of CA. While Sweden has a slightly higher MA, our goal here is to make sure that our first sales rep in the Nordics has as few barriers in her way as possible. After all, we must be mindful that even though she is just one rep, we want to set her up for success with our company and make it painless for her to hit her quota.

Not only that, but we've learned that if we sell software in Sweden and we force the customer to pay in our currency (USD) instead of theirs, their total cost will be higher because they can deduct the software in taxes if they pay in Krona, but not if they pay in a foreign currency. Part of the reason we're winning in many parts of the world is that we offer more attractive pricing options than many of our competitors do. If we choose to sell in Sweden without adapting further, even though our price will remain the same, we'll be inflating the total cost our customers must pay there (see Table 8.2).

Our account renewals team flags that we don't yet actually have an easy way to let our customers choose to switch their currency at the time of renewals in an automated way. This means that even if we add support for the Krona later, our renewals team will have to go back and manually change the preferred currency in all of those accounts in Sweden that were originally paid in USD. Our billing team also warns us that the current billing system we use doesn't support Swedish Krona. They'll be switching to a different system soon, but their preference would be to roll out Krona later, after they have fully switched over to the new system.

As a result, our leadership team ultimately decides that we'd like to hire someone in Sweden eventually, but for now, we choose to hire our next rep in Finland.

TABLE 8.2. How to Think Through Various CA Metrics

Category	Sub-Category	Question to Ask	Sweden	Finland
Payment	Currency	Do we offer the currency of the local market?	No	Yes
	Payment type	Do we support the most common payment types of the local market?	No	No
Product	Pricing	Do we offer pricing that was developed with this market in mind?	No	No
	Packaging	Do we offer any packaging or bundling that was tailored based on this market's unique needs?	No	No
Language	Proficiency	What percentage of people in the local market speak the home market language that we already support?	High	High
	Degree of localization	To what degree have we localized the experience for the local market?	High	High
Presence	Employees	Do we have employees who live in this market?	No	No
	Office	Do we have a physical office facility in this market?	No	No
	Partners	Do we have partners or resellers in this market?	No	No
Operations	Type	What is the level of economic development?	High	High
	Ease	How does the country rank for ease of doing business?	High	High

Make It Easy for Customers to Pay the Way They Prefer

Many companies are somewhat naive in thinking that they can go into markets without making it easy for customers to pay them. While it's true that many companies transact only in one currency, their success will be limited if they are unwilling to reduce payment barriers.

I cannot stress enough the importance of offering local currency and payment capabilities to reduce friction and make it easier for your customers to actually transact with you. This is the heart of any business relationship. You don't want a friction-filled payment experience to be one of the things that stands out in your customer's mind.

If you fail to do this, much of the other work you have done to expand internationally will be in vain. All the money you spend to bridge a localization gap, the care with which you recruit local partners, and so on, are worth nothing if your customer gets frustrated when it's time to check out and decides it's not worth the hassle to do business with you after all.

Will your Swedish customers be willing to pay in US or EUR? Perhaps, but in a world where your performance metrics matter, you can assume higher sales velocity in any market when you offer the local currency.

The CA analysis also helps you unearth more detailed and practical concerns from around the business that could influence the timing of your decisions. Everyone on your team is a fan of growing more in Sweden, but when you consider what's in the best long-term interests of Swedish customers, the operational complexities with your billing system and adding a new currency that have to be considered, it might be faster to hire a sales rep in Finland to hit your near-term goals.

The reason I've chosen an example of two markets that are so similar is that it highlights the importance of thinking through the details before you make decisions that can have cascading impacts on the operational side. You want to align everyone around international expansion goals, and it's important to set the tone up front that you're all part of one team, and that considerations like this can help your company make decisions that might seem small initially but can generate (or prevent) consumption of your internal team's time and resources.

Consider Both Local Product-Market Fit and Local Go-to-Market Fit

Another way to think about customer addressability is to consider whether your company has both product-market fit locally, and what I refer to as local "go-to-market" fit. In my opinion, too many companies focus their time and energy on product-market fit alone, neglecting the importance of how they go to market locally. Without adapting their go-to-market approach to suit the needs of the local market, they typically find that their efforts stagnate as they attempt to address a larger share of the local TAM, mostly down to the simple fact that they are not going to market in a way that makes sense for the local market. Instead, they tend to operate with a company-first mentality, seeking to leverage a global approach. But leaning too heavily on a single global approach and not allowing room for adaptation and flexibility is ultimately what slows growth down in new local markets. A balance of both is required.

For many companies with a digital model, product-market fit is actually easier to achieve locally than go-to-market fit can be, especially in the early years. Often, product requirements are quite similar, at least on the surface, from one market to the next. This is obviously not the case for highly regulated industries where the product must operate differently according to local laws and regulations. In general, both product-market fit and go-to-market fit get harder to achieve as you go deeper into a market, because of the maturity and needs of the types of customers you are able to reach at each stage.

Local product-market fit is vital, but so is local go-to-market fit. True local success requires a balanced blend of the two.

There is another important reason I encourage business leaders to think about the concept of customer addressability early, and to think about not *if* your company will flex and adapt as you go into new markets, but rather *how* you will do so. The reason I encourage this flexible mindset from the start is that adaptations become more and more important as you go deeper into any new market. Otherwise, your growth will slow down at some point because your company isn't doing enough to adapt.

As Geoffrey Moore explained in his book, *Crossing the Chasm*, most companies will hit a slowdown in growth at some point due to a gap—or a chasm—in the market when it comes to technology adoption. If you're leading a tech company, keep in mind that going into each local market is like crossing the chasm, over and over again, one country at a time. This means your company will be learning what it means to leap the chasm, make adjustments, and create a complete product in each local market. This does not apply to only product, but rather to go-to-market approaches as well, especially in companies with a strong product-led growth aspect to their business.

Companies tend to assume they can leverage much more of their domestic success than they really can. They fail to see that they've actually already highly localized their product and their go-to-market motion—by orienting their entire business toward one market, their home country. When they see success globally, they think, "Our playbook works everywhere!" In reality, it's only working to reach a small percentage of the TAM, usually the early adopters.

There is often a mismatch between where the company actually is in terms of crossing the chasm in a local market and where the leadership team might believe they are. Local teams are usually much more realistic in terms of where the company is in terms of local brand awareness, local suitability, and local adaptations. However, they often don't speak up when the company sends a strong message that they are committed to a global playbook. This is the classic challenge companies face when growing globally—finding the perfect leverage between their global initiatives while allowing for local autonomy.

The deeper you go into any local market, the more adapta-tions your company will need to make to truly achieve your full potential there. If your company is unwilling to be flexible and adapt, you'll only be able to reach a small percentage of the TAM in that country.

As you go into new local markets, you can still leverage the majority of what you do. A small degree of adaptation can go a long way. Often, companies can be change-resistant and inflexible, citing that they don't wish to introduce complexity and would rather keep things consistent globally. In reality, making small adjustments doesn't always have to be that complicated. There is wisdom in keeping things simple, but as a business leader, you also need to be on guard that this isn't being used as an excuse to prevent the company from meeting the needs of local markets, which will slow down your global growth.

Why don't more companies simply adapt to local market needs? Often, people assume it will be harder than it really is and may be averse to change. Many people at your company will be change-resistant and reluctant to truly adapt locally to the degree that is required. It can be scary and daunting for them to think about. Fortunately, many of the game-changing adaptations with the highest impact might actually be quite simple to implement. For this reason, it's critical that you make it clear to employees that certain adaptations for local markets are essential. Don't be silent on this matter, or you'll be quietly enabling them to stay in a stance of inflexibility, which can lead to stagnation and thwart the innovation you need.

As your company grows, you want to keep things flexible and adaptable no matter what. My suggestion is, instead of looking at local adaptations as a headache or something that can wait until later (when it might actually be too late), try to get your employees to see local adaptations as something that strengthens the entire company, making your business more flexible and adaptable as a whole. The truth is, it makes you stronger internally, while enabling the company to reach its full global potential. Taking a moment to enable and consider local flexibility is vital, like stretching before running. Whether your goal is to sprint or to run a marathon, prepare your muscles in advance to do the best possible job— no matter what local race you happen to be running.

REVOLUT CASE STUDY
Product-Market Fit, Country by Country

For companies operating in the fintech and banking spaces, going into new markets often carries a heavy up-front load. But the hardest part of expanding into any new country might not actually be navigating the complex details of a brand new banking system, or even mastering the local financial regulations. Rather, the hardest part might just be achieving true product-market fit.

"To nail your product-market fit, you have to listen extremely closely to what the customer wants, and that's going to be very different in each new market" explains Yuval Rechter, General Manager of Revolut in the United States. "The customer's needs might look the same at first, on the surface. But the details of how your local customer thinks about it differently, at deeper levels, is what ultimately matters."

This belief in truly understanding the local customer has served Revolut very well as the company has entered many new markets with great success. Today, the UK-based company is highly global, operating in 36 countries with 37 global offices and more than 5,000 employees. Revolut facilitates 250 million transactions in 120 currencies globally per month. It's actually an "international-majority" business—out of 25 million customers Revolut has globally, 75 percent are based outside the United Kingdom.

(continued)

(*Continued*)

Revolut is fairly new in the US market, having begun their soft launch in the market in April 2022. Fast forward six months, and they had 150 employees in the United States and half a million customers. And while they have much bigger plans for expansion in America, they made an intentional decision not to go too quickly into the market, before gaining a deeper understanding of American customers. "Your company's first impression in any new country needs to be a good one," points out Rechter. "You can't rush it if you want to succeed in the long term."

"The landscape in the United States is completely different from the United Kingdom," explains Rechter. "The market in the US is highly competitive, so American consumers nearly always expect to see reward programs and cash-back offerings, and we've also learned they want personalized products. But one of the biggest differences is the importance of credit in the United States. People really care about their credit scores and how their financial lifestyle affects that. None of these things are of high importance to customers in most European markets, and they're certainly not common in the United Kingdom."

Traction, not initial speed of entry, is the top priority for market entry in cases like these. In a crowded and mature market like banking in the United States, having a deeper understanding of the customer is necessary to achieve true product-market fit, which will ultimately give Revolut the traction it needs to gain market share. Adapting their products for the US market might take longer, but it's absolutely necessary for the long-term success they seek. "We couldn't just rush into the US market with the same product offering we have in the UK," explains Rechter. "Too many companies do that and fail, exiting the market as fast as they entered it."

"You hear a lot about American companies going into other markets and making mistakes, but it's easy to see how European companies can make similar mistakes going into the US market from abroad," points out Rechter. "That's why it's so important to learn as you go. Otherwise, you'll miss out on understanding local pain points and how they define value locally. If you fail to pick up on local nuances that matter to customers, you could easily end up with a product that's too generic."

Rechter says that one major hurdle is building an internal company culture where there is high awareness that local market differences are real. "This is one of the biggest challenges companies face when going global," he points out. "You have to give local teams autonomy, while freeing up resources from central teams. It's not easy to build company-wide recognition that every local market has its unique differences, along with a high level of trust in the local teams to do what is best for the company overall."

Revolut has a unique competitive advantage in this regard—its extreme cultural diversity within the company. Incredibly, more than 80 nationalities are represented among their employee base, which means that more countries are represented internally than the company has a customer presence in. Such a non-homogenous base of employees with knowledge of many countries, languages, and cultures is more likely to jump over the hurdle that Rechter warns about. High-functioning global companies are filled with employees who can spot local differences, act on them, and customize for each market, fortifying the company from within while it continues on its path to going global.[3]

Key Takeaways

- In the early days of your expansion, consider picking a "good fit" market based on the barrier to entry, like Netflix did, especially if you're operating in a highly regulated industry.

- Pay attention not only to your product-market fit for new local markets, but your go-to-market fit as well.
- The more geographically and culturally distant a market is from your founding location, the more important it will be to pay close attention to customer feedback in the new local market.
- Cultural distance barriers between you and your customers can be overcome by changing your internal company culture and the composition of your employees. Make sure you're hiring for international experience and cultural knowledge, as Revolut does, from the earliest possible phase.

III

GO GLOBAL FROM WITHIN

9

BUILD A GLOBAL-FIRST CULTURE

As we've discussed, companies are going global earlier and earlier in their evolution as a business. But what if you were global from the start? Increasingly, companies are starting out this way.

The number of companies that are "default global" will continue to grow over the years. If you're an early-stage founder or your company is still small, you have a great opportunity to be global from your earliest days and should consider this approach and whether it might work for your business.

But if you've already started a company, or you are a business leader at any company, it's not too late to infuse a Global-First mindset into your business. In fact, I would argue that the reason "default global" or "global native" companies hire in multiple markets early on is *because* they have a Global-First mindset. This should be a source of relief, because no matter how big you are, and no matter how far your journey has gone, it's never too late to become a champion of Global-First thinking, so you can build it into your culture.

There is nuance to what Global-First actually means, and employees can get it wrong, almost always with good intentions. Here are some key things that can help you understand what Global-First really means, and how to think about building this mindset at your company.

Global-First means creating things with global in mind from the beginning, but unfortunately that isn't enough. That's just the first step (see Table 9.1).

The next step, and what really makes something Global-First, comes down to (1) the details of how you execute to enable local flexibility, (2) the ability of teams to quickly connect with each other across geos, and (3) letting the local leaders make decisions about what is best for their markets, while ensuring they have the resources they need to turn plans into results.

Global-First also means connecting the dots, thinking through all the various pieces of how a given initiative will succeed—or fail—in each market based on a company's ability to connect these internal dots. Global-First not only means thinking globally from the start, but considering how to execute locally too.

Ultimately, make sure you advocate for everyone in your company to think globally, but execute locally. This is a hallmark of Global-First thinking and can make or break the success of your global business.

True global success requires finding the right balance between thinking globally and executing locally. Nailing execution in any market requires giving local teams the autonomy and resources to drive results.

Infuse Global Thinking into Your Culture

Many business leaders want to take their companies global and get their employees to jump on board. So, how do you transform your organization in a way that truly fuels your global growth? To bridge the gap between strategy and execution, you'll have to focus on changing the way your employees think. If you don't, they'll do what is natural—develop a product, process, or program with their home country and culture in mind, instead of designing for a multimarket use case from the beginning.

TABLE 9.1. Examples of Business Situations and Applying Global-First Thinking

Business Situation	Why It's Not Global-First	How to Make It Global-First
Your company is setting up a new team that will carry specific global targets. The new manager says, "Let's hire a team member in every country so we can be really Global-First!"	Not all countries matter equally, and working across too many time zones and cultures too quickly can make it difficult for the team to achieve stability that can set you up for long-term global success Problem: Assuming every market is equally important at a given point in time.	The new manager speaks to each regional leader, asking if the new team's work will be relevant for their markets in the early days, explaining the global goals of the new team. Using this input, the manager decides to hire one person in each major focus market, with 50 percent of the new hires in the domestic market, aligned with the company's current revenue targets.
Your company is launching a new video-based training for all employees companywide. The team rolling out the training says, "Let's be Global-First and localize this into all the languages of all of our offices so all employees can have equal access to the content!"	Perhaps the content itself is not relevant for each market, or perhaps video-based training isn't even necessary or the best way to convey the same information for each market Problem: Assuming the best way to reach employees in one market is the best way to reach them in another.	The team talks to a few key leaders in each major market, asking them if this is the best way to get the information across. One leader wants to just use the content in English without localization since most employees there speak English. In another market, the content is too culturally charged, so the leader suggests converting it to slides, which the leader herself offers to present to the team and include in local new hire training going forward.
A new product marketing campaign is being released soon for prospective customers in all markets. The team rolling it out says, "We've already been thinking Global-First, so this campaign is already localized and ready to go, globally!"	Unfortunately, some of the local sales teams are not ready to sell the new product in their markets, because no compensation plan has been created for their regions. Only the domestic team has an actual comp plan that motivates them to sell the new product. Also, many of the enablement materials that support this campaign have not been localized either. Problem: Global teams not communicating holistically about initiatives with regional teams.	The product marketing team asks the regional marketers about the forthcoming campaign, prior to localizing. They learn that there is no budget for the enablement resources to be localized just yet, and the sales operations team also needs more time to figure out local comp plans. They decide to create a calendar in which they can stagger the launch and time it in certain markets later than others, given the need for the other global teams to have other pieces sorted out so the campaign can achieve maximum success in each local market.

Remember, globalization tends to be a largely invisible business process at most companies, so it won't become a topic unless and until you make it one. As such, you'll have to think like a marketer: brand it, give it a name, and start communicating, then repeat your message in many different ways until it sinks in.

To really get people to embrace global thinking and make it part of their everyday work, you'll need to come up with a term that works at your company. For example, when I first came up with the notion of "Global-First," my team and I began to repeat this message everywhere we went. We started recruiting internal influencers to help us spread the global message along the way. We set up a Slack channel for the people we saw as global ambassadors, so we could collaborate in getting the word out. I started posting on our company intranet often, promoting the term wherever I could, and asking others on my team who felt similarly inspired by this mission, to do the same.

Plant the seeds of what you hope will eventually become a meme—or a viral concept—as the company grows. Over time, these efforts multiply and become amplified as you grow. If you're at a smaller stage as a company, you're in luck, because you're still in time to start making globalization a mantra and weaving it into your culture. And even if you're bigger, you can still have an important influence by branding this initiative and rolling with it from there. Better late than never!

You don't necessarily need to use the term "global-first." That worked for me, but it might not be the right term for your business. I've heard of some companies that use "global-ready," "think global," and so on. That said, if it does work for you, feel free to use it. There is plenty of other work to do to take your company global, without having to reinvent the wheel on this one.

Create an International Steering Group

One way to highlight how important globalization is for your business is to create an international steering group. This group will be responsible for identifying challenges to your international businesses and creating plans to solve them. Here are some suggestions for how to set up and manage a steering group during some of your pivotal years of international expansion.

1. Give someone full ownership of the initiative.

When you first create an international operations and strategy function, you likely won't need a team of people. At first, you might have just one headcount who spends approximately one-third of their time every month preparing for and organizing the monthly steering group meeting. The meeting will likely require more than one hour—it might even be two to three hours long initially. It may require a huge amount of preparation to ensure its success. In the early days of expansion, you may find that an international steering group requires a large amount of time from your executives, so it will be critical that everything runs with extreme efficiency. If you already have a format or a model that works well for your executive team meeting, consider whether you might borrow much of the same structure that your executives are already comfortable with.

This position requires experience, excellent communication skills, and the ability to work cross-functionally. I would not recommend trying to outsource this type of coordination work, nor would I delegate it to an admin-level person only. The ideal person to lead it either has ample business experience working in various functions or has an advanced business degree such as an MBA.

2. Have an influential "decider" chair the meeting.

When you first begin the meeting, you'll need to partner with an executive sponsor, such as a VP of Operations or a Managing Director for International to come up with the monthly agenda in order to shape the meeting.

While everyone can voice their thoughts in this type of meeting, it's very important to have someone, ideally a C-level person with budgetary authority who can work cross-functionally, who can make decisions during the meeting, or easily get answers that can enable decisions. This most likely will be a CEO, COO, or CFO, but it could also be an international sales leader if they are properly supported by all functions. Also, having the right person chairing the meeting ensures that everyone wants to be there, prepares adequately, and shows up on time.

3. Get the right people to attend.

Whoever is steering your international business, usually a sales leader, is a mandatory attendee. The other people you add to the recurring invite list will need to be able to make important decisions about your international business. So, you'll want to ensure you have the right people in the room. Who the "right people" are depends greatly on the topics you'll be discussing and the goals of the meeting itself. If your primary goal is alignment, you'll simply need to ensure you have representatives from all groups that need to connect.

You might need regional representation, functional representation, or more commonly, a mix of both. Ideally, the group will consist of leaders responsible for driving growth and alignment. In some cases, and depending on the size of your company, this might include your CFO, CRO, COO, CSO, CMO, or CCO. You'll need people from various functions attending for the group to be successful at making decisions and clearing the path for growth. Every business will require a slightly different structure and format for these meetings.

Typically, you'll have a core set of people attending as well as special guest presenters on different topics of interest. Usually, the guest presenters will be people working in a local office or on a specific initiative of importance for your international business.

4. Decide on the cadence.

If you're in a SaaS business or one that monitors monthly recurring revenue closely, the obvious choice will be to meet monthly to discuss the previous month's performance. Timing the meeting right may be tricky, due to so many busy executives attending. Try to develop the calendar one year in advance and send out all the monthly invitations at once to ensure the time gets blocked.

One tricky part of scheduling this type of meeting is, of course, conflicts with time zones. Set a good example of being Global-First and avoid asking your international employees to work outside of their normal workday. Make sure your executive sponsor is supportive of your international business and voices a strong preference for adapting to meet the needs of other time zones. You'll be setting the tone from the top down, so everyone feels that it's important to make this level of commitment too.

5. Come up with a simple format.

Your meeting will likely consist of three main sections: monthly performance, discussion topics, and "quick hits," or important updates that require knowledge sharing but not discussion.

For the monthly performance section, you can operate primarily from just one slide that shows all your key international performance metrics at a glance, indicating which ones are on track, off track, or borderline. Devote the time to any that are off track. In advance of the meeting, the organizer should gather the metrics from the various teams in question (Marketing, Sales, Customer Success, Finance), double-check them, and ask questions about any areas of importance.

As you're doing the performance metrics, whenever you appear to be off track in a given area, connect with the regional leader who owns the metric in question in advance of the meeting, and ask them to be prepared to speak briefly as to why the metric is off track that month during the performance section. This will give your top executives, such as your COO and CFO, a chance to ask further questions and try to gauge whether the issue is truly problematic and warrants further inquiry or actions.

For the discussion topics section, get input or meet with a few other key collaborators and come up with three or four topics of approximately 20 to 30 minutes, enough time for a brief presentation and discussion leading to decisions. Examples of discussion topics included things such as:

- Whether to accelerate hiring in a local market
- Marketing strategies being piloted in a local market
- Sales channels being explored in a local market
- Blockers in a local market (as identified by performance metrics)
- Local office location selection
- Localization initiatives

You may also wish to experiment with having international customers attend so that you can talk with them, but just remember that the logistical challenges of doing this can be quite disruptive to your agenda. You may also wish to rotate the focus of the meetings, to discuss different key markets or regions separately, especially if they are of a similar size and stage. However, you'll likely want to focus more time and attention on the focus regions. You may find yourself frequently considering your agenda and updating the structure in order to yield the best results.

Lastly, you can cover any "quick hits," usually just five minutes each, no more than three slides. Often, the organizer of the meeting can quickly present these summaries, such as the status of a local office launch, or an update on something discussed in a prior meeting that was of importance for the group to know about.

6. Ensure accountability.

You may be fortunate when running this steering group meeting to find that many executives attend who are highly respected, so everyone attending the meeting feels it becomes important to attend. Executive presence in the room also helps ensure that people go out of their way to follow up on key action items. You might be surprised how receptive people are to supporting your international growth.

That said, people are busy! Make sure that whoever runs this meeting documents the discussion with detailed notes and assigns follow-up actions to everyone who needs to take action, along with a clear deadline. You may publish these on your internal Wiki to encourage transparency, and so others know that they have eyes on their actions.

Ultimately, an international steering group is a powerful way to drive a Global-First culture. By getting executives involved with your international business, you send a loud message to others about its importance.

Make Global-First a Part of Company Culture

Here are some other ways you can help make Global-First part of your culture:

- **Training.** Add the concept of Global-First to your new hire training, so that everyone knows what it means and why it matters.
- **Incentives.** Consider creating an award to recognize employees who showcase global thinking. When you create such an award, this usually becomes a popular program that can enable you to motivate employees and get them excited. You might not need to do this forever, but it really helps to drive visibility for globalization in the early years.
- **Mixers.** Make sure your employees from different parts of the world can easily connect with each other and meet virtually. Create a space for individuals to form relationships and learn about employees in different offices. For example, you can create a mixer program to connect employees who work in various locations. It can generate some fun anecdotes and relationships among your employee base, while broadening the mindset of those who haven't had a chance to travel to those locations.
- **Opportunism.** We've already talked about the importance of aligning international strategy with corporate strategy, but I also

want to highlight the importance of being opportunistic. At various points in time, there will be talking points, initiatives, and priorities that become almost viral in your company. If you see a great way to connect globalization to any of these, do so. You'll often need to explain to people how one thing connects to the other.

DASHLANE CASE STUDY
Headquarters Are a Thing of the Past

As companies grow across borders and remote work expands, the notion of "headquarters" has begun to stretch. Many companies establish a regional headquarters in every part of the world as they expand internationally, adding physical offices in those locations. Others adopt a "dual headquarters" model, in which members of the executive team and large numbers of employees are based primarily in two core locations. However, these models surfaced during times when remote work was far less common than it is today.

Dashlane, a software company offering subscription-based password management, has taken things a step further. Founded in France in 2009, the company's first CEO moved to New York when raising the company's Series A funding round. As the company grew both globally and in revenue, they made a unique choice—to forgo the notion of a global headquarters entirely. Today, with 17 million users and 20 thousand business customers in 180 countries, this strategy appears to be paying off.

Despite having its origins in France, the majority of Dashlane's customers and employees today are not located there. The company has workers in Portugal, France, Hungary, Canada, Romania, Spain, the United Kingdom, and the United States—the country where most of its customers are based today.

Not only does Dashlane intentionally have no headquarters location; the company sees it as an advantage, and a vital part of their culture. Ciara Lakhani, Chief People Officer at Dashlane, believes that not having a headquarters sends a fundamental message of inclusivity to global employees: "People are very sensitive to having practices from a different country feel like they are imposed upon them, so you need to be really intentional to avoid that as much as possible."

Dashlane's geo-agnostic headquarters strategy also shows promise in terms of minimizing some of the thrash that employee-facing teams experience as their companies expand globally. "There's a lot in the profession, even beyond laws and different health insurance and retirement plans, that really differs by country," Lakhani points out. The barriers associated with different countries are real enough already. Declaring a single location as the company's sole nexus of decision making can add unwanted complexity to an already challenging picture.

Lakhani elaborates, "In a post-pandemic world where people know they have more choices, is there really any direct benefit to declaring a place in the world as your headquarters? I can't think of one that outweighs giving a company access to the best possible talent and giving employees the reassurance that even if their personal circumstances change and they need to move to another place, they won't be at any disadvantage."

Indeed, Dashlane's practice of being intentionally polycultural and distancing themselves from being tied to just one primary geography is the way of the future for many companies, especially for the next wave of global digital natives.[1]

10

AMPLIFY LOCAL
CUSTOMER VOICES

One of the most important ways you can drive international expansion and globalization at your company is to amplify the voices of your local customers. This is particularly important because for many companies, their largest market also happens to be their home market.

You run the risk, when you're highly concentrated in just one market, of living in something of a bubble, disconnected from the needs of your customers from outside your home market. It's relatively easy for you to meet with customers in person, or at least virtually in the same time zone. This can make you fall into the trap of thinking that your home-market customer needs are reflective of all your customer needs. It can be eye-opening when you realize that you need to adapt and fill quite a number of gaps in your local customer experience.

Domestic Voices Often Drown Out International Ones

Not listening to voices from outside our home market and our native language is a common challenge for most companies headquartered in any large market where everyone speaks a common language. Most companies can only address so many opportunities at once, and it only makes sense for most businesses to start where you have local ties and relationships, especially in the founding years.

If you're headquartered in a large English-speaking market, such as the United States or the United Kingdom, you can easily fall into what I call the "English echo chamber." In this space, you hear the same things being repeated back to you over and over, shaping the way you think about your customers and how your business addresses them. This is natural, but it can cut you off from the rest of your customers.

One analogy to help you understand why this is such a common problem is to think about the choices you make when listening to music. When you listen to playlists or the radio, are you listening to music in your own language? Most likely the answer is "yes." Or are you purposely seeking out music in languages you don't understand, and from countries you've never visited? To do that, you'd have to go out of your way. That music probably isn't at your fingertips. It isn't played on any of your local radio stations, so you can't even access music from other countries with analog. You can leverage digital technology and use your phone or laptop to go online, but you might not even know where to begin to search for it. You also might not have the ability to type in a language that uses non-Roman characters to even type in a keyword to begin with.

This is why most businesses don't solicit local customer feedback in any large-scale or meaningful way. It's very difficult! When you can access such large populations and market share with one language only, it seems easy and natural. You don't have to go out of your way. The problem is that it can mislead you into thinking that customers outside of the markets that speak your language have the same needs and think the same way. This can lure you into a false sense of security, making globalization seem less urgent and important than it really is. A common refrain you might encounter in this situation: "But we're already so successful around the world! The need to adapt further is simply overblown." This is an example of not wanting to hear the messenger, let alone listen to local voices.

Herein lies the risk. By not tuning in early enough to key local markets, many businesses eventually hit a slowdown in growth because they're not listening carefully to their international customers early enough in their market expansion. The advice in this chapter will help your company avoid reaching that point of stagnation, using customer insights to fuel your business, so that you can keep growing steadily over time without risk of slowing down.

Use a Combination of Quantitative and Qualitative Research

Many companies, especially at early stages, tend to lean heavily in the direction of either quantitative metrics or qualitative research. For digital-first companies, it's more common that they err on the quantitative side of the spectrum, simply because they have access to so much data. Rare is the company that strikes a great balance and uses both harmoniously, even though both are of great importance.

Qualitative feedback from local customers is hugely important, especially at the early stages of growing a business in a new market. From my experience, companies do not lean into this enough, but when they do, they find it incredibly insightful. One risk, however, is that executives become overly enamored with such feedback and lean into it a little too much, even if it's not reflective of the broader market. For example, some business leaders will claim they understand local customers, citing anecdotes based on talking to just one or two. They might also mention a regional leader who has given them a recommendation. While one-off anecdotes are helpful, nothing replaces gathering qualitative input in a structured way.

For this reason, I suggest that if you're gathering local feedback with a qualitative approach, such as interviewing customers or otherwise capturing their verbatim feedback, that you have a way of categorizing and coding this feedback, so that it moves from anecdotal to structured qualitative feedback. Ideally, you build this into your business so that it isn't just a one-off, but rather, a continued initiative.

On the other side of the spectrum, some companies lean way too much into their data, letting it dictate every move they make. As a veteran researcher myself, I love data and being able to quantify and understand the scope of a given business issue. However, quantitative findings can be useless without insights as to why the numbers paint the picture they do. When it comes to local markets, data can also be very misleading. The "law of small numbers" is important to be aware of, especially in the early phases. Sometimes companies get overly excited by a given performance metric, and I find myself trying to temper their enthusiasm.

For example, I was advising a company that got extremely excited about some of the early traction they were seeing with their online presence in India. They were developing a disruptive technology and publishing large amounts of content on their blog on a niche topic, for which not much online content was available globally. As such, they attracted traffic from English-speaking people searching for this content in many parts of the world. When they saw that 20 percent of their traffic was coming from India, they wanted to start hiring salespeople there.

Not wanting them to make a mistake, I shared some data so that they understood how big the population of English speakers in India is, and that the traffic could be more indicative of India's large population than their company's suitability for the market. I asked them if they had spoken with people on the ground in India to find out if their pricing and product really mapped to local market needs. They had not spoken to even one customer, but their reaction was one of surprise, even disbelief. How could I question such strong data? One of their team members even asked, "People are signing up there. What more proof do we need of product-market fit there?"

Fortunately, their executives shared other data to show that other metrics were off. Customer onboarding was taking longer, and product discounting was high, making the average deal size lower, which was a risk to their overall financial health and unit economics. They talked themselves out of intensifying their presence in India, but only because they had other metrics that painted a negative picture, showing they didn't actually have great product-market fit yet. Still, talking with customers might have accelerated their learning, or shown them what gaps existed in more tangible terms than just looking at the data, a lagging indicator of local market addressability in this case.

There is no replacement for talking to customers. They will tell you which aspects of your product are appealing to them and which might need more work. Never assume that data gives you the full story, especially if you're using it to drive international expansion decisions. Small decisions early on can snowball, and if you're not careful, they can defocus your team and lead you down paths that ultimately are not the most advantageous.

Prioritize Talking to Customers Directly

Can you get feedback from your partners and employees in local markets? Yes, of course—but be mindful that they are not your customers, and while they might be a good proxy, you don't want to lean too heavily on their feedback unless it's combined with direct customer feedback. The reason? They have their own filters that may taint local feedback, even if that isn't their intention.

I've noticed over the years that feedback from employees and partners in local markets is often useful for short-term time horizons, while feedback from customers will help you look at what it takes to succeed with a longer view. In other words, you'll likely need a mix of both, depending on the timeframe. If you're looking to solve an immediate need, listen closely to your local employees and partners, who can summarize the biggest trends and gaps they are hearing about in their day-to-day interactions. But if you seek feedback, for example, to build a product or make a bigger strategic bet in a local market, there is no replacement for talking directly to customers to understand their needs more closely.

Look at the Entire Customer Experience

In addition to gathering feedback in a more reliable way that leverages both quantitative and qualitative research, you'll want to look at the full customer experience. Some sources indicate that the quality of your product or service makes up as much as 50 percent of customer satisfaction, so there is no doubt you'll want to pay close attention to this. However, don't ignore other aspects of the customer experience, which may matter in equal measure.

Many product-driven companies focus heavily on measuring user experience or customer satisfaction within the product only. This is good information to have, but perhaps not reflective of the full experience. If you're in a B2B environment, for example, your user experience will help you measure usability / ease of use for the individual users, but perhaps the key decision makers involved in purchasing or renewal decisions are not actual end users themselves.

For example, a CEO at a small business of 100 employees might have strong influence over the accounting software her company buys from your business, and she might be the one authorizing payment, but perhaps only her Finance team members actually use the product daily and have logins. The company conducts an in-app survey regularly to measure user sentiment, and the users give the company high marks. But when the CEO gets the invoice, what if her experience with billing is shoddy? What if the payment bounces, and she has to waste time getting it solved? Just one small aspect of doing business with your company can paint a bad picture of your business in the eyes of the customer. This isn't to discount the importance of your product. If the users at this CEO's company are happy, she might be willing to overlook her pains in paying for it temporarily. But it's easy to see how, if you under-perform in just one area, your overall relationship with your customer can be at risk. Not only that, but you'll never know this area is problematic if you don't ask customers to rate their experience in this area.

Survey Customers and Measure the Gaps

To identify and fix gaps in your customer'experience, you can create a local experience survey program that would enable you to measure gaps in your experience for each local market. The concept helps you to understand differences by language, but later can evolve to enable you to look at experience gaps by country too.

Such a program basically consists of asking customers to rate their experience in a number of areas of the customer experience, identifying gaps, and fixing those gaps. Every year, you can run the survey, review the results, then meet with an executive leadership group to make decisions on how you'll address any aspects of the customer experience that your local customer feedback tells you need attention.

You can launch this type of program with relative ease. All you really need is a standard way of asking the questions, the ability to slice your data by country, and a clear way of communicating the results. Then you'll need to project manage any important initiatives that arise because of any gaps you uncover along the way.

When you create a local customer experience survey or insights program at your company, your goal is quite simple: to provide an equitable experience to your customers, no matter which market they are in, and no matter which languages they speak. I don't recommend surveying your customers in all countries of the world, especially if you have customers in markets that are not an important focus right now. Instead, focus on your key priority markets. Seek to provide an equitable experience to those customers.

To provide this equitable experience, you must both understand how you are perceived as a global company by your customers, and gain insights into their local experience. Those are the two main areas in which you'll seek to capture customer insights:

1. **Global company perception.** How do your customers think you're doing at understanding their country, and your effectiveness at covering their language needs?
2. **Local customer experience.** How do your customers rate their satisfaction with individual aspects of their experience with your business?

Measure the scores for each market and each category. When you repeat the survey, you can also measure the progress in each area.

You can easily measure how customers in local markets perceive your company as one that can meet their local needs. Ask them to rate their level of agreement with these statements:

1. "[Company Name] meets the needs of customers in my country."
2. "[Company Name] offers what I need in my language."

Then, measure the number of people who agree with the statements on a four-point scale: Strongly agree, agree, disagree, strongly disagree.

There are many variations you can use for these questions. For example, let's say you're a software company called DentalData and you target dental practices. You're based in the United Kingdom, and you have recently begun to sell into France. You can be more specific and say, "DentalData meets the needs of dental practices in my country." You can also indicate the country or language in the question directly in the survey itself, so that it's even more obvious, even auto-filling it based on customer records if the data is trustworthy. For example, "DentalData meets the needs of dental practices in France" and "DentalData offers what I need in French."

The output of this is that you'll have a clear score that enables you to compare satisfaction in your home market versus the new market where you seek to intensify your company's presence (see Table 10.1).

At initial glance, this data tells us that UK customers have a better experience than those based in France, which isn't surprising given that

TABLE 10.1. Hypothetical Customer Satisfaction Scores by Country

DentalData Customer Satisfaction France versus UK	France	United Kingdom
DentalData meets the needs of dental practices in my country	68%	72%
DentalData offers what I need in my language	58%	89%

the company is based in the United Kingdom. Overall, the company is doing quite well in the United Kingdom with most customers reporting satisfaction, and the gap between customers based in France and the United Kingdom is quite small. This seems to indicate that the company is doing a decent job in France but has some room for improvement. When it comes to language access, however, there is a bigger gap. Because the gap is large (31-point difference), it appears the product is meeting local customer needs in France, but the company needs to do more with localization.

Now that you have a method for collecting data on a country-by-country basis, you can compare local satisfaction better, but you'll need a way to know what is "good" and what isn't. Add up the number of positive responses ("strongly agree" + "agree") and divide it by the total number of responses to come up with a percentage. In other words, if 30 percent of your respondents said they "strongly agree" and 40 percent said they "agree," 70 percent of your customers in the local market are satisfied overall. Table 10.2 shows a recommended way to think about the scoring ranges.

You can also apply a stoplight system if that is common at your company. Good = green light or "go," Borderline = yellow light or "yield," Red = red light or "stop."

The rationale for these scoring ranges is that 70 percent or higher in terms of satisfaction levels is generally considered to be a "good" customer satisfaction (CSAT) score. And if your company is seeing nearly half of customers in any market report that they are not satisfied, you should definitely pay attention to local market performance and dig deeper.

TABLE 10.2. Customer Satisfaction Score Ranges and Actions to Take

Score	Meaning	What to Do
70% or higher	Good	Lean into what you're getting right in this market and see if you can replicate it elsewhere
65–69%	Borderline	Put this on your watchlist and come up with a plan of action to fix issues, ideally raising the score to "good"
64% or lower	Bad	Raise awareness of the problems and meet with the responsible teams. Come up with a clear plan of action and seek exec support to make changes.

However, I recommend that when you look at these types of scores, you don't just focus on moving a percentage upward. Instead, you'll want to look at each cohort in comparison with others. This will enable you to spot trends that are global in nature and areas of general risk to your business too. In addition, you'll want to focus on the year-over-year progress in each area. Let's take a look at a similar example of a year-over-year comparison for the same type of fictitious company, and what it might mean (see Table 10.3).

In this scenario, we can spot some interesting trends in the year-over-year performance when looking at regional differences. The country-based scores slipped slightly for customers in both markets, which might be indicative of a global trend. Perhaps the company is no longer serving early adopters, for example, and is targeting larger or more demanding customers in both markets. Or perhaps the company rolled out some new product tiers, and customers' unhappiness with this change is reflected in the scores.

When we look at the language scores, we can see that DentalData did a good job of narrowing the gap for French customers, and we can assume that they offered more, or the right type, of content needed in French. However, the English language score dropped, perhaps related to the product tier changes, and customers no longer being able to find

TABLE 10.3. Hypothetical Changes in Customer Satisfaction Scores

DentalData Customer Satisfaction France versus UK (Year-over-Year Comparison)	France		United Kingdom	
	2022	2023	2022	2023
DentalData meets the needs of dental practices in my country	68%	67%	72%	71%
DentalData offers what I need in my language	58%	78%	89%	85%

what they need in their language due to certain content being limited just for higher-tier users.

For this reason, it will be natural for your business to want to segment each country further, by tier, by product, by employee size, perhaps even by their account rep. While this type of analysis opens up possibilities, the numbers start to get small quickly when you segment even further, so be careful to watch for overall trends, and not to be too tempted to slice and dice with too much granularity, lest you overthink it.

Now that you have a general sense of local customer satisfaction, you can ask one more question of your customers in the same survey. Ask them to rate their satisfaction at each major area of the customer experience. This will enable you to produce a chart like the one shown in Table 10.4.

From here, once you have the more detailed scores, you can take the average across all areas for each geo, and then measure year-over-year progress. This will enable you to provide an executive summary of where the gaps are, so that you can rally your company around fixing them. Also, this will provide local leaders with much-needed insights into the various aspects of the local experience that might be broken (see Table 10.5).

Table 10.6 gives an example of the type of simplified scorecard summary you can provide. This is helpful to give executives a snapshot of your company's standing in the market and where things are headed.

Surveys are hugely helpful, and I suggest them as a quick and simple way to capture feedback that will enable you to measure customer

TABLE 10.4. Hypothetical Customer Satisfaction Scores by Experience Area

How Satisfied Are You with DentalData When You . . . ?	France	United Kingdom
Use the product	72%	85%
Visit our website	66%	77%
Receive marketing communications	67%	79%
Need quick answers in the knowledge base	51%	64%
Need training	47%	59%
Participate in the onboarding process	64%	70%
Interact with support	67%	80%
Interact with salespeople	62%	76%
Receive billing and invoicing communications	52%	71%
Renew your account	43%	65%

TABLE 10.5. Hypothetical Year Over Year Change in Experience Area Scores

How Satisfied Are You with DentalData When You . . . ?	France		
	2022	2023	Change
Use the product	73%	75%	↑ 2
Visit our website	67%	65%	↓ 2
Receive marketing communications	67%	62%	↓ 5
Need quick answers in the knowledge base	52%	65%	↑13
Need training	47%	56%	↑ 9
Participate in the onboarding process	56%	69%	↑13
Interact with support	67%	75%	↑ 8
Interact with salespeople	62%	81%	↑19
Receive billing and invoicing communications	48%	64%	↑13
Renew your account	45%	57%	↑12
Average	58%	67%	↑ 9

TABLE 10.6. Simplified Country Scorecard Example

France	
Net YoY change	↑9 pts
Most improved areas	Onboarding, Sales
Needs work	Training, Billing, Renewals
2023 score	67%
Compared to United Kingdom (69%)	2 points lower

satisfaction and compare it across different countries and languages. However, there are some important caveats you'll want to think through:

- **Phrasing matters.** How you word your questions can have a major impact on the results. Consider asking a few customers how they interpret the questions before you launch the survey more broadly to ensure you're capturing feedback on the things you want to know more about.
- **Translation is critical.** You can't just do this survey in one language if you're targeting people in multiple languages. The survey must be conducted in the language of your customer, and again, you'll want to validate that the way you ask the questions is truly getting at the issues you want to cover.
- **Cultural differences abound.** Even if customer satisfaction were identical in some markets, the scores would be different. This is because certain markets are notorious for behaving differently when using rating scales, no matter what they are asked to assess. Japan is a market that is notorious for low customer satisfaction ratings, even with native Japanese companies. Latin American markets tend to rate satisfaction high, even if they are actually unhappy with many pieces of their experience.
- **Local differences may appear too.** Even local differences can exist within the same country. In the United States, studies that look at CSAT ratings in various industries find that customers in southern

and midwestern states rate them more favorably than those on the East Coast, which tend to rate more harshly, no matter what the industry or company is. Certain gaps are natural.

- **Look at cohort composition closely.** If your business in one country looks dramatically different from your business in another, this might show up in your local customer satisfaction scores. For example, let's say you do not offer local pricing in Poland but sell only to larger companies there that can afford your product. Customers might rate you lower, not due to differences related to country or language alone, but because overall they have a very different profile than that of customers in other markets.

- **Involve functional and local leaders in the survey design.** If your initiative is a success, your company will begin using this data and reporting on it routinely. As such, involve your functional and local leaders as early as possible. Some will be eager to get this data; others might be worried about how it will reflect on them and their teams. The more experience you gain in this area, the easier it will be to build relationships and get everyone on board with the overall purpose.

- **Keep in mind that some areas naturally score lower than others.** Customers who absolutely love renewing their account or paying their bills are probably pretty rare, no matter what business you're in, what country they're in, or what language they speak. Don't be surprised if certain areas score much lower than others. It might just be harder to ever score very high when it comes to certain areas of interaction between you and your customers.

- **Watch closely for trends across all local markets.** One of the most interesting things that starts to happen when you look at this data across various markets and over a longer time horizon is that you can start to spot global trends that show up in all parts of the world at the same time. That's an exciting time, because it's reflective of the fact that you're becoming a truly global business.

- **Don't measure too often.** Some people ask if they should measure more than once a year. That's up to you, but in general I'm a proponent of measuring less frequently and gathering a larger sample size versus surveying more frequently and being overly reactive to insights from smaller cohorts. Making any major improvements in local customer satisfaction scores tends to take time. I also suggest measuring at the same time of the year if possible, and trying to achieve a similar sample size each time you collect this data.

Lastly, a more advanced exercise is to survey your local customers and ask them to rank the importance of different aspects of their experience. This enables you to provide a weighted average score. In the example provided above, all areas weigh equally, and the average provides a snapshot. But ultimately, using local customer feedback to actually understand which areas matter most to them is an even better option if it's possible, and can lead to more relevant findings.

I am generally a fan of doing this to uncover local views toward the categories that we might think are important but might matter more to certain geographies than to others. Just keep in mind that how they evaluate the importance of a certain aspect of their experience can also relate to other factors, such as the department they work in, their title group, company size, and much more. For example, a CFO might rank the invoicing part with the highest importance, while a user not involved in purchasing might rank the product as the most important part.

Keep Your Eye on the Prize: Continued Improvement

Gathering this amount of local customer data can seem a bit overwhelming to companies at first, so it's your job to ensure that everyone keeps their focus on the broader business goal. You're seeking to improve your customer experience overall. What this means is that you should look at the raw numbers, but what matters much more is the comparative data, especially when looking at progress in the same market, year over year.

While we'd all love to see high scores in all areas and in all countries when we measure customer satisfaction, keep in mind that some degree of variation is natural. Instead of being frustrated by this, approach the results with curiosity. Make it clear to local teams that you're not out to blame anyone, but that this tool will help your company understand local differences, to strengthen the global whole.

Give your team permission to focus on creating an equitable experience that keeps getting better for customers in each local market with time. Forcing an identical experience on customers is generally a failure to acknowledge their local reality, so don't think you are doing them a favor by deciding on their behalf what should be most important to them. Instead, let customers tell you what they need, focus on delivering on those needs, and watch as what at first appears to be a local adaptation benefits your entire global customer base and your entire company.

Key Takeaways

- Getting feedback from customers in new markets is vital, because these usually provide the highest growth uplift to your business while older markets become more saturated with competitors. Don't short-change this effort due to the magnetic pull of your customers in your largest market.
- Don't over-index on quantitative feedback. The data won't tell you the reasons behind the behavior, and likely the numbers will be too small in the early days to be reliable anyway. There is no replacement for talking to customers directly, especially in the early stages, before you decide to intensify.
- Measuring across the full customer experience gives you a more complete picture of global customer experience. Cutting the data by country and language can help you identify which functions might be suffering globally versus which ones are symptomatic of the fact that you're ramping up in a new country.

11

BUILD A GLOBALLY EQUITABLE ORGANIZATION (GEO)

The best motivation for building a global company is that you want your customers to be successful with your company, without geography becoming a barrier that prevents this from happening. Customers are happy to pay a price in exchange for value that they believe is fair. That's where creating an equitable experience comes in.

If your customers in one market receive less value than those in another, they perceive your offering differently than what you actually intend. This is not only unfair to them, but also to you and your employees, and it will hurt your business in the long run. For this reason, even if you're already having success as a global company, that's simply not enough. To sustain your success for the long term, you'll need to build not just a company that is global, but a globally equitable organization (GEO).

To ensure that your customers have an equitable experience with your business no matter where they are based, you'll want to strive to make local experiences equitable, but not necessarily identical. In fact, where many companies go wrong is that they try to enforce a cookie-cutter approach onto all their markets in the name of "global leverage." But in doing so, they miss out on the importance of local adaptations that are required to ensure their customers are equally happy with the value they're receiving in their local market, even if they define and derive that value in different ways. Table 11.1 gives some examples of what this means in practice.

Encourage your employees to flex their creative muscles when thinking about what strategy is best for a new local market. The temptation is always to do the same thing, all at once, in every market. This is a natural inclination, but one that can ultimately create too much work and require more resources than what you really should be investing in a new market at the stage where your business is within it.

Introducing the GLOBE Principles

To truly create an equitable experience for your customers, you will need to focus as early as possible on becoming global and driving the mindset that will get all of your employees to focus internally on keeping the global momentum going.

Here are five guiding global principles your company may want to adopt, from the top down, bottom up, and across every function of your company, along with a mnemonic, GLOBE, to help make it easy for everyone to keep them top of mind:

Geo-agnostic
Linguistically inclusive
Operationalized
Balanced
Empathetic

Let's look at each of these principles and explain why they matter.

Geo-Agnostic

Most companies start in one market and later go into another. This is natural and the way business has typically been done. It maps to a time when the world was less connected. Now that more companies are digital

TABLE 11.1. Examples of Equitable Adaptations for Local Markets

Customer Experience Area	Current Home Market Approach	Local Market Approach Initially	Why It's Globally Equitable
Marketing	A large website that has built up over the years with large amounts of content	A microsite with just the core content that enables customers to understand the parts of your offering that matter most to them	You didn't create such a large website for your home market overnight, so you don't need to localize all of it. Start small in your local market and focus on their unique needs.
Sales	A large inside sales team that sells directly to customers	A local partner that resells and implements your products	You can't recreate the trust you have built up in your home market over many years quickly in a local market. Going in with an already trusted brand makes more sense.
Product	A fully featured product offering with numerous tiers, bundling options, and pricing add-ons	A lightweight version of your product that removes many features that won't work in the local market for a single lower price point	Your business mix is more complex in your home market than in a new local one. It's often better to customize than to sell things that they don't need or cannot use.
Support	An in-app support tool that offers automated support via a chatbot with the option to reach a human 24/7	A local phone number that routes to a local human rep only during local business hours	It might be logistically easier to launch in the local market with human support reps than to localize your chatbot, and you can build greater brand trust with humans initially. Cost of human talent is lower in the new market anyway.

or even digital-native, it's more important than ever not to be tied to just one geography, or to become too deeply rooted in just one part of the world. Instead, you want to operate in many markets at once.

Geo-agnostic speaks to what you believe in. If you believe your initial market is where you're headquartered, and that you'll address other markets later, that's one approach, but it's not geo-agnostic from the onset. However, if you believe your market is the world from day one, you'll think, act, and grow in a way that naturally enables multiple markets. Having a geo-agnostic mindset from the beginning makes it easier to become a multimarket business.

Being geo-agnostic is a lot harder than it sounds. Many of us have views that were shaped by experiences working in, living in, or visiting other countries. Through the media, we are surrounded by stereotypes about people in different countries and who speak other languages. Being geo-agnostic also doesn't mean burying your head in the sand and believing that all markets are equal or the same. Markets are different, and being geo-agnostic means acknowledging these differences while staying open to learning more about these places as your business grows, and as your strategy warrants moving into them.

Linguistically Inclusive

Language is a hugely important part of building a truly global company. A single word can make or break a relationship, both in and outside of business. The words you choose to convey messages about your brand to your customers and prospects are a large part of how they view your company and what makes up your identity in the long run. Too often, we forget in our day-to-day work that a brand goes far beyond a corporate style guide, logo, and predetermined color palette. It's how your customers perceive your business. Language is one of the biggest ways you shape your brand identity.

So, when we talk about linguistic inclusion, we cannot just talk about making sure information gets translated into the other languages of your local customers. That's like saying to a marketer, "Can you write up the

'About Us' page? Anything in English will do." It's not enough to swap words in one language for words in another. The people translating your content need to know and understand your brand. Otherwise, they simply cannot convey it into the target language, and the ultimate message you're driving can get lost.

In addition, where language is concerned, linguistically inclusive also means accessible to people with varying language needs, including disabilities. Your definition of linguistic inclusion could also consider plain language, meaning that you consider the needs of people with varying levels of literacy, non-native people who speak the language with lower levels of proficiency, and so on. For this reason, you'll need to always build things in a way that makes language easy to access and, ideally, easy to localize.

Operationalized

When we use the term "operationalized" in the context of being a global company, we mean that a global mindset is fully baked into your company's business operations, from the way you hire to the software you buy, from the processes you design to the people you invite to participate in them. Everything you do should be done in a way that supports international expansion and does not create blockers for your international customers.

To have an impact on your global trajectory, global thinking should be hard coded into as many aspects of your business as possible. Sometimes tech company leaders are taken aback by this idea because agility matters hugely too. Operationalizing a global mindset does not mean you need to be dictatorial to your employees or reduce autonomy, but rather that you want a global mindset to naturally seep into everything you do so that it becomes repeatable and can grow with you as you scale.

Balanced

International growth is often described as a juggling act, especially when you're focused on many markets at once. It's true that many international leaders have to keep a lot of balls in the air simultaneously. But ideally, if you take a balanced approach, you can build in stability to reduce the chaos and keep everyone focused.

Balanced does not mean that all markets matter equally. Quite the contrary. It means making sound choices that won't destabilize your business. You have a fiduciary responsibility to your employees, shareholders or investors, and ultimately the customers who depend on your business to survive and continue to deliver your products and services to them. As a result, you cannot commit to all local markets at the same time. You must make choices and focus.

For growing businesses, it's important to avoid spreading your resources too thin and into too many markets simultaneously. Don't try to grow in too many places at once. You can certainly grow in many markets at the same time, but focus most of your efforts on intensifying your company's presence in just a few key markets at the same time. Otherwise, your results can become diluted.

One analogy I like to use when helping business leaders with this topic is the difference between throwing one large rock into a pond of water or throwing the same weight in tiny pebbles. If you opt for the pebbles, the effects on the surface will soon disappear and not even be noticeable soon after they hit the water. If you opt for the rock, you'll see ripples that are far greater and more noticeable for a longer period of time. The same is true in business, but it's especially true when you're trying to build a strong local brand in multiple places at once. Put your weight behind fewer local markets for more impact. The rest of the world will still be there for you later.

A critical place where balance also matters, and where you'll need to revisit this concept over and over as you go global, is in the allocation of resources. Going global means continually rebalancing your resources to ensure you are funding the investments that matter for each geography at every stage of growth. This is an area that is commonly neglected at many companies, and dropping the ball on this can lead to infighting, accusations of unfair expectations placed on local teams while domestic teams receive a bigger share of the pie, and discontent among employees.

But beyond all the internal consternation and unwanted distractions your company will face if you don't distribute resources fairly across markets, the bottom line is that you're not doing your very best to ensure your local customers get what they truly need. Keep a close eye on how you balance your budget geographically and build in ways of tracking your commitments to each market from the earliest possible days. In addition, make sure you continually evaluate the geo-distribution of your headcount and external spending allocations as your company grows. Don't just do it as part of annual planning. Geographic composition of your customer base can change quite quickly, sometimes even in the space of just a few quarters when you're at earlier stages of growth.

Empathetic

Finally, you'll need a hefty dose of empathy for your customers in local markets. Empathy means you can understand their perspective and know what it's like to walk in their shoes. Most companies do not take the time to truly do this. Instead, they assume that the challenges some customers face are the same all of them do, in all markets. Many companies just fail to understand that where your customers live shapes everything they do and how they perceive your business.

Where you live in the world, and where you're from, may form a huge part of your company's identity. Local laws, local politics, and local economic trends shape business and how it's conducted in every market. Even things like the local weather and religious holidays can translate into financial impact for your customers, and for you. If you have doubts about this, just consider the impact of Christmas and Thanksgiving on spending habits in the United States. Similar phenomena exist in every country and shape every industry. We're just oblivious to these things if we're not close to our local customers. This is why empathy is a hugely important part of building a global company.

Table 11.2 shows an example of simple questions you can ask, and encourage your employees to ask, when you're launching any new undertaking at your company. Asking these questions is a simple way to help you figure out how well your initiative will scale globally.

If you get into the habit of putting these five simple principles at the front and center of your thinking, you'll naturally be driving a Global-First mindset.

TABLE 11.2. Questions to Ask to Apply the GLOBE Principles

Guiding Principle	Question to Ask
Geo-agnostic	Is this project designed around the needs of customers in just one market, or is it inclusive of multiple geographies?
Linguistically inclusive	Have we considered the different language and literacy needs of customers in the local markets we serve?
Operationalized	Have we accounted for local differences with our plans, so we can prevent friction for local teams when it's time to execute?
Balanced	Are resources, especially funding and headcount, aligned to support our priority markets?
Empathetic	Have we talked with customers and/or leaders of our local markets to ensure we are taking their needs into consideration?

CANVA CASE STUDY
Lead with a Globally Minded Mission

Most companies are founded with an initial focus on their domestic market. Digital and online companies are born to be global someday, in that even if they are created with a domestic orientation, they can more easily reach international markets early in the life of their company. But rare is the company that actually starts out with global as a stated goal from day one, orienting themselves toward the entire world from their earliest days.

(continued)

(*Continued*)

Canva, a graphic design platform with a $40 billion valuation, is one such rare and special company. The business was started in Australia, but the founders had a global vision from its very inception. With more than 20 thousand employees around the world, 100 million users, and an estimated US$1 billion in annualized revenue, Canva's global approach has clearly served it well.

Most companies begin talking about global markets only when they start to see international revenue increasing. One of the most interesting but little-discussed aspects of Canva's global success is how its global vision manifested from a much earlier point in its history—in the form of globally diversified investment money going into the company to fuel its growth. Unlike most tech companies, Canva teamed up with venture capital firms on three different continents, receiving funding from companies based not only in Australia, but in the United States and Germany as well.

Canva's experience is proof that if you have a global vision from the earliest days, including at the initial fundraising stages, you can build a global company not only *for* everyone in the world, but *from* anywhere in the world. But you can only do that if you hire the right people along the way to help execute that vision. While the majority of the company's employees are based in Australia, every single person who joins the Canva team becomes part of their mission to make a positive impact around the world.

The stated mission of Canva has remained largely unchanged since its earliest days: "To empower everyone in the world to design anything and publish anywhere." Note the words "world" and "everyone" and "anywhere" that all seek to reinforce the global nature of the company's mission. For example, Canva's software is available in an incredible 100 languages, and employees often remind themselves that English is "just another language" to ensure their decisions never become rooted in Anglocentric thinking.

There is great power in building a company with a mission that draws in likeminded, purpose-driven employees who want to make a global impact. The mission literally shapes every decision that a company makes, from the investors Canva works with, to the people it represents within its software platform, and the way Canva team members think and execute within the scope of their work each and every day. In this regard, Canva really is a shining example of a "born global" business that can serve to inspire other founders and business leaders to build a global company, no matter where they are based in the world.

Key Takeaways

- In the digital age, nearly any company can be global, but this alone isn't enough. The bar has been raised, and the best-of-breed global companies aspire to build globally equitable organizations (GEOs). This ensures that their employees, customers, and users all have equitable experiences without geography being a barrier to access.
- To build a globally equitable organization, you have to be geo-agnostic and language-inclusive first and foremost. But you also need to operationalize Global-First thinking, balance your resources, and build empathy with your local customers. These are encompassed in the GLOBE principles.
- There is no better way to inspire your employees to build a global company than to make it a part of your stated mission. Take a hard look at your mission statement to make sure it truly reflects the global potential your company has to offer the world, as Canva has successfully done.

12

HIRE FOR INTERNATIONAL KNOWLEDGE

Most companies orient their planning and processes around the needs of their home market. In the early stages of growing a business, it's hard enough to nail product-market fit. So, when they eventually go global, they find that their company is unprepared on many levels to meet the needs of an entirely different market. You can fast track some of the organizational learning—and minimize the global growing pains—if you hire the right types of employees from the earliest possible stage. The sooner you do this, the faster your company will evolve into a global business.

Start by prioritizing international experience, ideally as part of the hiring process, and your company will naturally have a strong global mindset built into its DNA. Even if you don't plan to go global until much later, hiring people today who have a global perspective can future-proof your business and ensure that you prevent common stumbling blocks that can slow you down later. Here are some of the main categories of people you may want to consider hiring as early as you can to ensure you have less friction taking your company global when you decide to do so.

Immigrants and Refugees

To build a sustainable business that can thrive in international markets, seek to hire people who were born in, and ideally raised in, a country other than your company's home market. These individuals bring a very important perspective into your business. Because they come from another cultural context and have knowledge of another country, they bring this into your business every single day. Unlike a skill that can be taught in a course, or a mere framework that anyone can learn in business school, employees who have a global outlook on life itself don't have to struggle to bring this perspective into their work. It happens automatically, and because it's so much easier this way, everything they touch ends up being more global friendly. This prevents friction later as your company grows into new markets.

There is plenty of research documenting the importance of immigrants in business. In the United States, immigrants represent 27.5 percent of entrepreneurs but only 13 percent of the population. An entrepreneurial mindset is more common among immigrants; they contribute to US entrepreneurship at twice the rate as native-born Americans do. The same phenomenon occurs in countries all over the world, with immigrants contributing in outsized ways to entrepreneurship in most economies.

Not only that, but companies led by immigrants do better in terms of employment growth, according to a Harvard Business school study. William R. Kerr and Sari Pekkala Kerr, the authors of the study, found that immigrant-led companies grow faster and have higher chances of survival long term than companies led by native-born Americans. As William Kerr remarked, "The very act of someone moving around the world, often leaving family behind, might select those who are very determined or more tolerant of business risk." Many of these same qualities are reasons you should hire immigrants to help you build your business too, especially if you seek to build a global company.

What I have personally noticed is that immigrants bring another dimension to the workplace and are additive to the culture of any team. On some of the teams I have managed in the past, 95 percent of the individuals were either immigrants living outside of their home country or have experience living for an extensive period of time in another nation.

Children of Immigrants

Often, the same growth mindset and entrepreneurial qualities that immigrants bring are passed on to their children. Many children of immigrants speak the language of their parents, and many immigrated themselves at a young age. Many have also moved around quite a bit, especially in their earlier years, promoting adaptability, an understanding of the role of inclusion, and tolerance for change.

What matters isn't how many years they spent in each place, but rather, how much contact they've had with another culture and language. If a person grew up primarily speaking another language at home or spending a lot of time with elder relatives who did, or visiting their parents' home country frequently, this tends to yield excellent and ongoing international experience that can be valuable in a business setting.

Workers Who Speak Other Languages

Learning another language typically means learning about another culture or part of the world. Individuals who speak other languages can be highly additive to your business, even if they never get the chance to use those language skills at work. Any exposure to another language opens one's mind to another way of thinking. You might find someone who graduated from a bilingual immersion school, for example, who never has set foot outside of their home country. Even without direct experience in other countries, the exposure to another language can be hugely helpful, as these employees are more likely to exhibit the traits that will help your company go global.

Another great thing about people who know other languages (or have at least attempted to study them) is that they know there is plenty they don't know. Learning a new language can be a humbling experience because it forces you to start from scratch. Also, language reflects culture, so knowing other languages means you are more likely to be able to understand diverse viewpoints. As your company expands internationally, the ability to see things from multiple and varied angles becomes more important.

Employees with International Work Backgrounds

If you are lucky enough to find people who have actually lived and worked in multiple countries, even if they are native-born citizens of your domestic market, consider these employees as valuable potential contributors to your business too. Their experience is hugely valuable because it's often directly relevant to your business. Often, these individuals don't prioritize (or even list) these experiences on their resumes. They might see their international experience as irrelevant to what you're hiring them for if it's not an international role. Even so, they will bring an important lens to any job they do while at your company and can be a tremendous asset once it's actually time to scale internationally.

Indeed, if you do find people who have worked at global companies, even if from within a domestic market, or better yet, have been active members or managers of distributed global teams, make sure to hire them if they are a good fit for a current opening. These individuals are very likely to have knowledge and experience that will help you significantly as you grow globally. The more of them you can hire before you need their global experience, the better they will know your company, and the more positive, global-friendly choices they can help you make earlier, in order to support your expansion later on.

People Who Demonstrate Global Curiosity

There are a great many people out there who might not be immigrants or have any direct experience with another country or language in the workplace or at home, but who demonstrate global curiosity in other ways. If you encounter a candidate who mentions they have traveled or have a hobby that is linked to other countries or cultures, this can only be a benefit. Sometimes they have volunteered through a nonprofit overseas and have had to do their best to be scrappy in challenging situations (Peace Corps volunteers are excellent examples). Or maybe they volunteer for a charity that connects people from abroad with specialist medical care in your home country.

Whatever the case may be, take note of people who simply care about the rest of the world or take an interest in engaging with countries outside your home market. This usually means they will also care about your international customers, without you having to invest as much time and energy in selling them on the idea.

Simple Ways to Enable Cross-Geo Connections

In the early days of your international expansion, you may want to create a simple award for employees who exemplify Global-First thinking. For example, every quarter, you can select a winner to travel to work from an office location of their choice for two weeks. This might be viewed as a major perk for employees, and it encourages people to undertake more cross-geo projects to help them build stronger bonds between countries where you operate. It also plants seeds and enables you to spot talent who are enthusiastic about international initiatives for later on. You might even find some of your future leaders and stars this way!

Encourage your executive team to travel to other locations too. You might also consider holding executives accountable by listing the names of which people at the VP or C-level are traveling to each international office. This can serve to highlight who is pulling their weight for your business internationally from the highest levels of your company, but it also generates a somewhat competitive spirit among many executives who might feel a bit more compelled to visit each office if they see their peers' names appearing regularly.

Today, in our post-pandemic reality and in the age of hybrid work, the need to travel to physical offices is lessened, but you can never underestimate the impact of spending time in a local office with the people on your global team. Especially when executives visit, local team members love to have the chance to engage with them, share their thoughts, and make important connections. Leaders, in particular, should make the effort to spend time on the ground with local employees—and with customers—whenever they can reasonably do so.

That said, there is no reason anymore to limit these informal one-on-one interactions to just occasional in-person office visits requiring travel to other countries. You might consider creating an international buddy program to enable people from other countries to connect for a quick "watercooler" type virtual chat with each other across geographies, levels, titles, and functions. Your primary goal with this type of simple program is to create more intracompany links for your colleagues in other countries who might feel isolated from your headquarter location.

Never underestimate the impact of small, unscripted, casual meetings between colleagues in different geographies! After all, it's not always easy to feel connected when you're one of the early employees in a local hub at a global company. In many ways, it's like being part of a start-up within a scale-up. While it's hard to recreate a watercooler effect in a globally distributed work environment, these kinds of simple efforts can go a long way to help a company improve its level of global cohesion from within.

Aim for Global-First Leaders at the Highest Levels

Building your company with global in mind as early as possible not only means hiring people with international experience. It also means making a concentrated effort to put these globally minded leaders in key positions. If you want to achieve a high level of global success early in the life of your business, aim for a high percentage of people with international perspectives in leadership roles.

In my opinion, having worked previously as a consultant with many large tech firms over the years, and having observed how executive attitudes toward going global can affect the rest of the company, the depth of international experience on an executive team can give your company a more global trajectory from your very earliest days, even when international growth is not yet a top business priority. In addition, many of the executives you will hire later on, including your board members, should ideally have extensive experience working in global companies, immigrant backgrounds, or both, as part of the mix of things you are looking for.

On the flip side, don't be concerned if you don't have many people on your team with international experience today. You can always hire for that! Indeed, not every person with strong international experience is suited to every company culture or can thrive in key leadership positions over the long haul. However, as your company grows and evolves, you can certainly make international experience a top priority, and a complement to other needs your business has, as you fill important roles on your team.

There are many benefits to prioritizing international experience as you round out your executive team and board, and as you bring on new leaders. What I have observed is that people with a global mindset tend to want to work with others who have one too, on top of any other skills they are seeking, even if they are not consciously aware they are doing so during an interview process.

The key takeaway is this: If you can infuse Global-First thinking at the highest levels of leadership in your company, including your C-level leadership positions and board members, your company will be many steps ahead of where you would otherwise be on the path to achieving global success.

ZOOM CASE STUDY
Global Growth with an Immigrant Mindset

One noteworthy example of an immigrant helping drive global business success from the top down is Eric Yuan, a China-born entrepreneur who has achieved incredible success with his US-based business Zoom. Yuan embodies persistence, having been denied a visa eight times before finally being given a chance to move to the United States in the 1990s, landing a job as one of the first 20 employees at WebEx, and later founding Zoom, a company that is today worth many billions of dollars, where he remains CEO.

But persistence isn't the only thing Eric Yuan cites from his immigrant experience as a key factor for his company's success. In an interview with Forbes, Yuan explains that hard work was a default expectation for him as an immigrant. As he explains, "I wanted to survive and prove myself. The only way I could do that was to work harder than other people. Compared to [native-born Americans], I didn't have a choice."

Yuan also managed to use his immigrant background to help put obstacles in perspective. Even when venture capital (VC) firm after VC firm turned him down when trying to raise money for Zoom, he wasn't deterred. He had already been through so much, having moved to a foreign country alone, learning a new language, and becoming a successful engineering leader at WebEx. As he explains, "I thought, 'When I came here, I had nothing, but I survived.' And when VCs weren't interested, I also thought, 'Yeah, that's okay, I will find a way to survive.'"[1]

Even if you're not an immigrant founder or CEO, the lessons Eric Yuan learned often apply for many immigrants who may seek leadership roles and opportunities in your company. After all, before he founded Zoom, Eric was a major contributor to WebEx, leading their engineering function, and helping them achieve significant growth. For this reason, don't overlook the power of hiring other growth-minded,

(continued)

(Continued)

> entrepreneurial people with immigrant experience for roles throughout your company. Often, the "forced growth" these individuals have already experienced personally leads to the very mindset that you need among top talent to grow your business into new markets globally.

Going Global Is Always a Team Sport

While having globally minded leaders is important, and hiring people with international experience is critical, support for Global-First needs to come from everywhere in your company, at all levels, for one very simple reason: When you begin to scale your presence in any market and hire your local leaders, you need to seek out multipurpose business leaders who are capable of building out a new start-up, locally, within a scale-up environment.

Your local leaders have a lot in common with entrepreneurs or founding teams. In fact, they are much like leaders who start up a new business unit or a major product line within a larger enterprise (commonly known as "intrapreneurs"). Those types of leaders who are hand-picked to innovate within a new business unit are notoriously isolated by design, with the goal of giving the leader the necessary autonomy to innovate without the constraints and bureaucracy of the larger business.

Interestingly, this very same phenomenon is what you'll witness when you hire country managers or landing leaders in any major focus country where you decide to put feet on the ground. Those individuals who help you scale your local market expansion have to behave like entrepreneurs in many ways, but they still need internal support. Just like the leader of a business unit, they must balance their entrepreneurial skills in building out the new local business, while simultaneously leveraging internal resources from central teams. The difference is, local leaders are not isolated by design, but by the fact that this isolation quite literally comes with the territory. And unfortunately, most companies tend to underestimate how isolated their local leaders actually feel, especially in the early days of scaling your presence in a local market.

To help your local leaders drive your business in each market, you'll need to give them access, collaboration, and support from others at your company. This sounds much easier than it is! When teams work in isolation from each other due to time zone, geography, culture, and language, the distance suddenly becomes very real. No matter how globally interconnected we may think we are, proximity bias sets in. People who simply don't see each other or communicate with each other very often won't naturally see a need to collaborate with each other unless they are told it's a top business priority to do so.

As you scale, you'll need local leaders in each market who focus on building out the business to map to local needs as best as possible, constantly seeking the best balance between the local autonomy they need and the places where they can find leverage globally. But their ability to access those places of leverage will depend directly on how many Global-First employees you have supporting them, in every function at your company. If you put a local leader in a situation where they are not supported by Global-First counterparts in every function, their leverage disappears, and they can become isolated and frustrated. This combination of local leaders and Global-First colleagues is the recipe for success when you're scaling globally (see Table 12.1).

One of the hardest things for your employees to remember is that they need to continually create pathways and relationships to local leaders and local customers, looping them into their communications, in order to ensure the company is not making decisions with unintentional proximity bias toward their domestic market. It's all too easy for colleagues to believe they are doing the right thing "globally," but they tend to forget that their view of the world is tainted because of a very natural proximity bias toward the local market they happen to be immersed in.

Remember, any decision that does not factor in the unique needs of local markets is not a Global-First decision. It might be a global decision, if you force it upon all markets, but it won't be Global-First. Your domestic market is just one market of many, and it's important for all colleagues your local leaders rely on to remember that. This is

TABLE 12.1. Aligning Local Leaders and Global-First Colleagues

	Local Leader		Global-First Colleague
Primary orientation	Geographic		Functional
Typical location	Local market		Domestic market
Main priority	Scaling the company's presence locally	← Alignment →	Supporting other business goals
Budgetary authority	Needs access		Enables access
Involvement in key decisions	Wants to be included		Seeks to include

why instilling a Global-First mindset companywide is of such vital importance.

Key Takeaways

- The best global companies are made up of internationally minded employees. Prioritize international experience in your hiring decisions but instill a Global-First mindset in every single employee, at every level.
- Country managers and local leaders are the champions who drive your business in local markets, but they will only succeed to the degree that their counterparts in other locations make Global-First thinking a priority at your company, so set the tone from the highest possible levels of leadership.
- Take a lesson from Eric Yuan of Zoom and know that immigrants often have a growth mindset hard-coded into their DNA. Even if many of your leaders are not from another country, you can still bring this mindset into your business by hiring people who will champion the international cause, to let it inspire people at your company from all backgrounds.

13

MULTIMARKET IS THE NEW MULTINATIONAL

International expansion is no longer the domain of big companies only reserved just for a special league or class of companies. Going global doesn't have to be just for the fastest-growing companies either, nor are their "secrets of overnight success" always the best advice to lean on. After all, the quickest growth isn't always the most sustainable, and going global is an ongoing commitment. Adding revenue at the fastest possible pace is not always the wisest move and can send you down a path of not being able to grow sustainably in the long term.

That said, my goal with this book, and the information I've provided to you throughout it, is to help you understand that taking a company global can be accessible to anyone who wants to do it. It is not just for the widely known brands or the fastest growing. Going global, quite simply, is something available and achievable for every entrepreneur, every business, every company who seeks customers in other markets.

You don't need to be a multinational to go global these days. What you do need is to have a multimarket mindset, in that you're solving for more markets, sooner, to enable your company to go faster in more markets later on, at a time when you become ready. By adopting this mindset and making it part of the way you operate, you'll build a business that can intensify your presence in more places when you decide to do so. But if you don't have that mindset early, it can be harder in today's reality to infuse it into your business later.

International Expansion of SMBs and Why It Matters

Small and medium-sized businesses (SMBs) are major drivers of most economies worldwide. SMBs account for 70 percent of all jobs, 99 percent of businesses, and more than 50 percent of GDP in high-income economies around the world. The shift to digital that we've been witnessing now for decades is only set to continue, with online customer bases growing even in categories that were traditionally offline. The pandemic has fueled this further. Increased digitization has led to increased globalization.

SMBs are currently undergoing a new wave of digitization, which is being quickly followed by a subsequent wave of international expansion. Digital business begets global business. While long underway, this particular wave is starting to pick up momentum. Many smaller and local businesses had less urgency to digitize in the past than they do today. But now that their eyes are open to the possibilities, they're bringing their businesses online even more, adopting software, and starting to see opportunities to expand their presence to more customers in different geographies and languages.

Global Growth Is within Closer Reach Than Ever

While I love to see companies pursue their global ambitions, I'm also a firm believer that not every business should focus on going global, or at least not at every stage of growth. Timing is key. Some businesses simply aren't ready. They need more time to solidify their offering in one market first and may never have the need to expand beyond that. There have been times when I have advised leaders to avoid adding the complexity into their business that going global would entail, based on what I've learned about their goals, challenges, and current state.

One thing that I strongly believe is that the secrets of going global should not be just the domain of big companies who can hire some sort of "global guru" to guide them along this course. The hunger and drive to go global is often more important than any other factor in making international expansion actually happen. While hands-on experience is helpful, every person who is an international advisor or consultant today started without that experience at one point in their career. They usually learned the ropes the hard way, by doing a job and learning about international expansion directly from local customers in one market at a time. You and your team can do this too.

If you can't access or hire people with specialist knowledge in international growth right now, don't despair or think that you can't build a global company without this type of expertise. Going global is a team sport, after all! Don't underestimate your organization's capability to learn what it takes to be a global success directly, by listening to your customers first. This is more powerful than what any international business specialist can tell you—and in fact, if they are good, it's one of the first things they'll advise you to do. It might also be one of the services they'll offer you, simply helping you understand what your customers in local markets really want and need. It's fine to hire people to help you with that, and this can put you on the fast track for expansion. But just know that this isn't your only option.

Remember that as a founder, entrepreneur, or business leader, you are operating from a special position. You already know your business and customers, and that is the foundation upon which all global success is built. Taking your business global is simply a matter of knowing a wider range of your customers and understanding how to adapt to reach more of them in new local markets. The key is to have a mindset of curiosity and an expectation that every market will have different needs to some degree.

Choose the Best Path to Take Your Company Global

Unless the product you're selling is extremely targeted to the needs of just one country, there are many paths available for your business to expand internationally today. If we look at successful global companies and how they are behaving in terms of when they decide to go global in the current digital age, we can identify three main profiles of companies:

1. Global-Native
2. Global-Early
3. Global-Later

Table 13.1 shows how these companies typically behave across different aspects of their business.

Make Your Company Stronger by Taking It Global

One of the least discussed aspects of going global is actually the one I believe is the most important, both for leaders who need to inspire their teams with a vision, and for the potential impact that businesses can have in the world. When you take your company global, you begin to democratize access to whatever benefits your business provides. If you're in business, you're offering something of value that someone wishes to pay for. This usually means that people in other parts of the world will also find value in what you're selling. It's just a question of how best to reach them, and how to adapt your offering to best meet their needs.

Once you begin an international expansion journey, this experience shapes the very core of your business and helps you transform your company along the way into one that is even stronger. Your business is going to change and evolve no matter what. Going global is just one of many directions in which it can grow, but an increasingly common and important one. The beauty of taking your company global is how much you'll learn, and how much you'll grow, sometimes in terms

TABLE 13.1. Types of Global Companies

Aspect	Types of Global Companies		
	Global-Native	Global-Early	Global-Later
Funding stage when going global becomes a priority	Seed or A round	B Round	C Round or later
Typical hiring approach	Hires in multiple countries from day one, will hire based on where they can find the best talent	Hires initially in home country but quickly adapts to hire in many different countries aligned with focus countries, including remotely	Hires mostly dictated by countries with physical offices; may be a late or reluctant adopter of remote work
Typical workforce	Remote majority	Hybrid	Office majority
Customer base	Has customers in more than one market from early in its history	Has customers in many markets from early in its history, usually pre-IPO	Has built up customers around the world over long periods of time
Time it takes to become truly global	Fast (shortly after founding)	Medium (within 5–10 years of founding)	Slow (11+ years after founding)
Mindset	Unleash the power of global growth from day one	Grow globally, but in a more controlled way	Grow globally eventually, but at a slower pace

of revenue, but often, in ways that are invisible but bring tremendous satisfaction:

- Bringing on new customers in countries you never thought would be possible
- Traveling to different parts of the world to better understand your true global market
- Creating employment opportunities for people in new parts of the world

- Understanding how your company meets an unexpected need in a new location
- Watching your customers engage with employees in languages you don't understand
- Knowing that the culture of your company now reaches into the far corners of the world
- Building something much bigger than you dreamed was possible

Taking your company global obviously benefits your company too. As you learn and grow globally, your organization will diversify and strengthen. You'll grow as a leader in the process. But those are really just side effects of the fact that you're going global, not the core reason for doing so. The bigger reason to take your company global is because you strongly believe you have something to offer out there in the world that can transform lives, shape ways of doing things, and bring joy, efficiency, and other benefits to your customers. If you lead with that type of grand, global vision, you'll be doing something of importance and value for your customers, your employees, and the world.

Key Takeaways

- Building a global business is not reserved just for certain sizes, types, or classes of companies anymore. Even a solopreneur can be "multinational" in the digital age. Multimarket companies are the way of the future for businesses of all shapes and sizes.
- Going global has a broader impact than just that of your business alone. Accelerating international commerce, especially that of small and medium-sized businesses, has major potential effects on the global economy.
- Companies go global in many ways, and at different phases of growth. It's never too late to take your company global, but in the

digital age, the earlier you build global thinking into all areas of the business, the easier the path will be.

- Taking your company global ultimately makes it stronger, more resilient, and more capable of innovating at the continuous pace that is required in today's business environment.

NOTES

Introduction

1. Stripe, "Global Natives," January 2019, https://stripe.com/newsroom/stories/global-natives.
2. Anish Acharya et al., "The Company of the Future Is Default Global," Andreessen Horowitz, July 20, 2022, https://a16z.com/2022/07/20/the-company-of-the-future-is-default-global/.

Chapter 1

1. Ian Harkin, interview by author, September 16, 2022.

Chapter 2

1. Faith Storey, "How to Expand Internationally—Lesson from VP of Growth @ LinkedIn," SaaStr., accessed December 30, 2022, https://www.saastr.com/international-expansion-lesson/.

Chapter 3

1. Peter Coppinger, interview by author, November 15, 2022.
2. Dan Taylor, "Airbnb Takes on Europe. Will It Revolutionize the Industry, Again?" The Next Web, July 6, 2011, https://thenextweb.com/news/airbnb-takes-on-europe-will-it-revolutionize-the-industry-again.

Chapter 4

1. Nataly Kelly and Jost Zetzsche, *Found in Translation* (Perigee/Penguin USA, 2012), 210–214.
2. Maggie Fick and Paresh Dave, "Facebook's Flood of Languages Leave It Struggling to Monitor Content," Reuters, April 23, 2019, https://www .reuters.com/article/us-facebook-languages-insight/facebooks-flood-of -languages-leaves-it-struggling-to-monitor-content-idUSKCN1RZ0DW.

Chapter 5

1. Nataly Kelly, "Looking for New Global Markets? Bigger Isn't Always Better," *Harvard Business Review*, November 9, 2020, https://hbr.org/2020 /11/looking-for-new-global-markets-bigger-isnt-always-better.

Chapter 6

1. Laura Warnier, interview by author, December 6, 2022.

Chapter 8

1. Louis Brenann, "How Netflix Expanded to 190 Countries in 7 Years," *Harvard Business Review*, October 12, 2018, https://hbr.org/2018/10/how -netflix-expanded-to-190-countries-in-7-years.
2. Netflix, Letter to Shareholders—Q3 2022, October 18, 2022, https://s22 .q4cdn.com/959853165/files/doc_financials/2022/q3/FINAL-Q3-22 -Shareholder-Letter.pdf.
3. Yuval Rechter, interview by author, September 29, 2022.

Chapter 9

1. Ciara Lakhani, interview by author, September 19, 2022.

Chapter 12

1. Joanne Chen, "American Dreamers: Zoom Founder Eric Yuan on Making His Mark on Silicon Valley," *Forbes*, July 11, 2022, https://www.forbes.com /sites/joannechen/2022/07/11/american-dreamers-zoom-founder-eric -yuan-on-making-his-mark-in-silicon-valley/?sh=329f97ed1f5b.

ACKNOWLEDGMENTS

The lessons shared in this book have been built over the course of my career, so there are loads of people who influenced it along the way. First and foremost, thank you to my husband and life partner Brian Kelly, for supporting me in my passion of helping people and companies connect across borders of language and culture.

To my daughters May and Eve, I'm sorry I couldn't put you on the cover of this book like you requested, but thanks for being my number one source of laughter and joy. Completing this book was made a lot easier thanks to those ingredients.

Thanks to my mother Linda Fletcher, and to my dearest friend Carla Lourenco Rodney, for both always striking the right balance between encouraging me to pursue whatever I happen to be passionate about, while gently reminding me not to overdo it.

This book would not be possible without the unrelenting, multiyear efforts of Scott Mendel, my agent. I truly value all your guidance, support, and encouragement not only for this book, but over the many years we've been collaborating.

To Neal Maillet, Jeevan Sivasubramaniam, and the wonderful team at Berrett-Koehler, thank you for believing in this book, for welcoming me into your community of authors, and for running a publishing house that aligns so well with my values as an author.

Special thanks to Brian Halligan (HubSpot), Tope Awotona (Calendly), Kathleen Mitford (Microsoft), and Mark Roberge (Harvard Business School) for supporting this book with your endorsements.

Thanks to Patrick Collison and the team at Stripe for helping me out with your research and data on "Global Native" businesses. Thanks also to Joe Schmidt at Andreessen Horowitz for sharing your research and thought partnership around "Default Global" firms.

My sincere thanks to Yuval Rechter and Mary Mitchell (Revolut), Peter Coppinger, Laura D'Angelo, Jenny Coppola, and Brad Coffey (Teamwork); Ciara Lakhani, Maayan Weiss, and JD Sherman (Dashlane); Laura Warnier and Karlijn Koekoek (GoStudent), and Ian and Sofia Harkin (Lottie Dolls). Thank you for allowing me to feature your experiences to inspire entrepreneurs at various stages of scaling and taking their companies global.

To my colleagues who work in localization and translation around the globe, thank you for all you do each day to make localization happen at your companies and for their customers, users, and visitors all over the world. Your work is often unseen by others, but always top of mind for me. I hope this book serves to elevate the localization profession even more. I'm so grateful to all of you for the support you have given me over the years and continue to give me as I seek to share what I learn along the way. Thanks also to Renato Beninatto (Nimdzi Insights) and Marjolein Groot Nibbelink (*Multilingual* magazine) for all your support of this book since its earliest days.

Lastly, thanks to mission-driven entrepreneurs and business builders everywhere. Your creative spirit and drive to innovate and develop something that grows, creates jobs, benefits your customers, and makes an impact on the world is a huge source of inspiration to me, and what ultimately drove me to write *Take Your Company Global*. I sincerely hope this book will help you do even more of that, but on a global stage, where I believe all companies doing good work, no matter where they hail from, can ultimately find their moment to shine.

INDEX

Information in tables is indicated by page numbers in *italics*.

ABOUT THE AUTHOR

 Nataly Kelly is Chief Growth Officer at Rebrandly, a global software firm with customers in more than 100 countries. She has previously served as Vice President of Marketing, Vice President of International Operations and Strategy, and Vice President of Localization at HubSpot. With more than a decade of experience as an executive at B2B SaaS companies, she has held executive roles in a variety of functions over the course of her career. Nataly is an advisor, coach, and champion of businesses going global, from start-ups to Fortune 500 companies. Based in the greater Boston area, she is a frequent contributor to *Harvard Business Review* and many other publications on topics of global business. Connect with her on LinkedIn, or at her blog, BornToBeGlobal.com.

Berrett–Koehler
Publishers

Berrett-Koehler is an independent publisher dedicated to an ambitious mission: *Connecting people and ideas to create a world that works for all.*

Our publications span many formats, including print, digital, audio, and video. We also offer online resources, training, and gatherings. And we will continue expanding our products and services to advance our mission.

We believe that the solutions to the world's problems will come from all of us, working at all levels: in our society, in our organizations, and in our own lives. Our publications and resources offer pathways to creating a more just, equitable, and sustainable society. They help people make their organizations more humane, democratic, diverse, and effective (and we don't think there's any contradiction there). And they guide people in creating positive change in their own lives and aligning their personal practices with their aspirations for a better world.

And we strive to practice what we preach through what we call "The BK Way." At the core of this approach is *stewardship,* a deep sense of responsibility to administer the company for the benefit of all of our stakeholder groups, including authors, customers, employees, investors, service providers, sales partners, and the communities and environment around us. Everything we do is built around stewardship and our other core values of *quality, partnership, inclusion,* and *sustainability.*

This is why Berrett-Koehler is the first book publishing company to be both a B Corporation (a rigorous certification) and a benefit corporation (a for-profit legal status), which together require us to adhere to the highest standards for corporate, social, and environmental performance. And it is why we have instituted many pioneering practices (which you can learn about at www.bkconnection.com), including the Berrett-Koehler Constitution, the Bill of Rights and Responsibilities for BK Authors, and our unique Author Days.

We are grateful to our readers, authors, and other friends who are supporting our mission. We ask you to share with us examples of how BK publications and resources are making a difference in your lives, organizations, and communities at www.bkconnection.com/impact.

Dear reader,

Thank you for picking up this book and welcome to the worldwide BK community! You're joining a special group of people who have come together to create positive change in their lives, organizations, and communities.

What's BK all about?

Our mission is to connect people and ideas to create a world that works for all.

Why? Our communities, organizations, and lives get bogged down by old paradigms of self-interest, exclusion, hierarchy, and privilege. But we believe that can change. That's why we seek the leading experts on these challenges—and share their actionable ideas with you.

A welcome gift

To help you get started, we'd like to offer you a **free copy** of one of our bestselling ebooks:

www.bkconnection.com/welcome

When you claim your **free ebook**, you'll also be subscribed to our blog.

Our freshest insights

Access the best new tools and ideas for leaders at all levels on our blog at ideas.bkconnection.com.

Sincerely,

Your friends at Berrett-Koehler

Certified

Corporation